# the ultimate book of
# mind maps®

# the ultimate book of

# mind maps®

**unlock** your **creativity**
**boost** your **memory**
**change** your **life**

# tony buzan

with susanna abbott, creative editor

 thorsons

Thorsons
An Imprint of HarperCollins*Publishers*
77–85 Fulham Palace Road,
Hammersmith, London W6 8JB

The website address is: www.thorsonselement.com

and *Thorsons* are registered trademarks of
HarperCollins*Publishers* Limited

The text in this book is based upon the material first published in the following
Thorsons titles: *Head First* (2000), *Head Strong* (2001), *The Power of Creative
Intelligence* (2001), *The Power of Spiritual Intelligence* (2001), *How to Mind Map*
(2002), *The Power of Verbal Intelligence* (2002), *The Power of Social Intelligence*
(2002), and *The Power of Physical Intelligence* (2003).

10 9 8

Mind Map® is a registered trademark of The Buzan Organization

Mind Map® illustrations by Alan and Emily Burton
All other illustrations by Alan Burton, Jeff Edwards, Peter Cox Associates
and Jennie Dooge

A catalogue record for this book is
available from the British Library

ISBN-13 978-0-00-721291-0

Printed and bound in China by
South China Printing Co. Ltd

This book is dedicated to the wonders of the brain
and to Mind Maps®, the ultimate mind-power tool.

# Also by Tony Buzan

# Contents

# Chapter Three

# Chapter Four

# Chapter Five

# Chapter Six

**Mind Maps for Everyday Success   184**

# Acknowledgements

With special thanks to my wonderful support team at Thorsons: Carole Tonkinson, Publishing Director; Susanna Abbott, Senior Editor, who has also helped me write and plan this book; Danielle Robertson, Designer; Jacqui Caulton, Senior Designer; Nicole Linhardt, Senior Production Controller; Liz Dawson, Publicity Director; Chris Wold, Sales and Marketing Development Director; Laura Scaramella, Rights Manager; and Belinda Budge, Managing Director.

A big thank you also to: Simon Gerratt and Charlotte Ridings for their editorial support; Alan and Emily Burton for their superb illustrations; and Caroline Shott, my incredible Literary Manager, whose energy and dedication constantly amaze me.

Finally, a special thank you to my home team: Lesley Bias for her 'flying fingers'; Vanda North for her tireless work promoting Mind Maps around the world; my brother, Professor Barry Buzan, for his decades-long support of me and the Mind Mapping concept; and to my mother, Jean Buzan, who has always encouraged me to pursue my vision for Mind Maps.

# List of Mind Maps

# Chapter Five

**Physical Fitness for Mental Power**

# Chapter Six

**Mind Maps for Everyday Success**

# Introduction

**Do you want to:**

Come up with innovative ideas and creative solutions?

Memorize information and recall it under pressure?

Set goals and achieve them?

Change career or start up your own venture?

Be an excellent time manager?

Run meetings with efficiency and ease?

Budget and plan to perfection?

Deliver excellent presentations with confidence?

Have more time for yourself and your family?

Enjoy success after success in your life?

If you have answered 'yes' to any of these questions, then you have the right book in your hands! Mind Maps are a unique thinking tool that will bring out your natural genius and enable you to shine in every area of your life. *The Ultimate Book of Mind Maps* is the definitive guide to using this remarkable tool.

**Chapter One, What is a Mind Map?**, introduces you to Mind Maps and how they work. It explains the basic Mind Map 'rules' and takes you step-by-step through your first Mind Map.

**Chapter Two, Know Your Brain, Unlock Your Potential**, digs deeper into the reasons why Mind Maps work and how they actually help your brain learn and think creatively. The better you understand your brain and how it works, the easier it is for you to help it perform to its best.

**Chapter Three, The Ultimate Success Formula**, looks at learning how to learn. It gives you a foolproof formula for learning and success that you can use in combination with Mind Maps. With the TEFCAS success formula and Mind Maps you'll always succeed!

**Chapter Four, Mind Workouts for Mental Success**, delves into the world of creativity and shows you how Mind Maps are the ideal tool for quality creative thinking. It also looks at how strong creative skills help your ability to remember things with ease, and gives you important memory principles that you can use with Mind Maps.

**Chapter Five, Physical Fitness for Mental Power**, highlights the importance of physical fitness for mental fitness. It looks at optimal ways of getting the right balance of exercise, sleep, and quality nutrition, and shows you how Mind Maps can help you achieve this balance.

Finally, **Chapter Six, Mind Maps for Everyday Success**, shows you just some of the infinite ways you can use Mind Maps in the workplace, socially, and in your general life planning. Use the Mind Map examples in this chapter to inspire you and your fabulous imagination, and you can be sure you will demonstrate your brilliance in everything you do.

Mind Maps wonderfully and dramatically changed my life for the better. I know that they will do the same for you, too.

Be prepared to be amazed – by yourself!

# What Is a Mind Map®?

*A Mind Map is 'the whole-brain alternative to linear thinking. [It] reaches out in all directions and catches thoughts from any angle.'*

Michael Michalko, *Cracking Creativity*

# Overview of Chapter 1:

**A Mind Map is the ultimate organizational thinking tool** – the Swiss army knife of the brain!

A Mind Map is the easiest way to put information ***into*** your brain and to take information ***out*** of your brain – it's a creative and effective means of note-taking that literally 'maps out' your thoughts. And it is so simple.

You can compare a Mind Map to a map of a city. The centre of your Mind Map is like the centre of the city. It represents your most important idea. The main roads leading from the centre represent the main thoughts in your thinking process; the secondary roads represent your secondary thoughts, and so on. Special images or shapes can represent sites of interest or particularly interesting ideas.

**Compare a Mind Map to a map of a city**

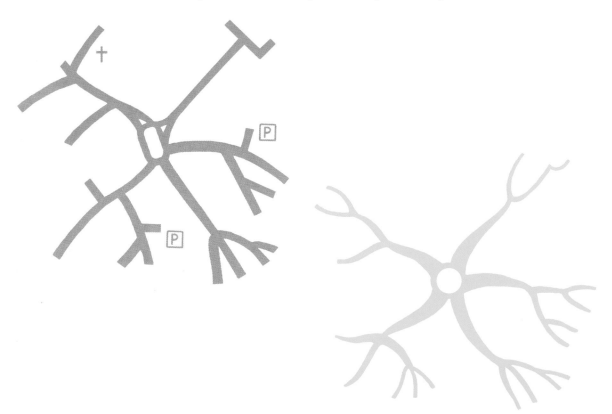

Just like a road map, a Mind Map will:

→ Give an overview of a large subject or area.

→ Enable you to plan routes or to make choices, and will let you know where you are going and where you have been.

→ Gather together large amounts of data in one place.

→ Encourage problem solving by allowing you to see new creative pathways.

→ Be enjoyable to look at, read, muse over, and remember.

Mind Maps are also brilliant route-maps for the memory, allowing you to organize facts and thoughts in such a way that your brain's natural way of working is engaged right from the start. This means that remembering and recalling information later is far easier and more reliable than when using traditional note-taking techniques.

All Mind Maps have some things in common. They all use colour. They all have a natural structure that radiates from the centre. And they all use curved lines, symbols, words, and images according to a set of simple, basic, natural, and brain-friendly rules. With a Mind Map, a long list of boring information can be turned into a colourful, highly organized, memorable diagram that works in line with your brain's natural way of doing things.

# How Can Mind Maps Help You?

Mind Maps can help you in many, many ways! Here are just a few.

Mind Maps can help you to:

→ plan

→ communicate

→ be more creative

→ save time

→ solve problems

→ concentrate

→ organize and clarify your thoughts

→ remember better

→ study faster and more efficiently

→ see the 'whole picture'

→ save trees!

According to Michael Michalko, in his best-selling book *Cracking Creativity*, a Mind Map:

> → activates your whole brain
>
> → clears your mind of mental clutter
>
> → allows you to focus on the subject
>
> → helps demonstrate connections between isolated pieces of information
>
> → gives a clear picture of both the details and the big picture
>
> →  allows you to group and regroup concepts, encouraging comparisons between them
>
> → requires you to concentrate on your subject, which helps get the information about it transferred from your short-term memory to your long-term memory

In *The Ultimate Book of Mind Maps* you will find many practical examples of how you can use Mind Maps to help plan and organize your life for maximum success, to come up with amazing, creative new ideas, and to absorb new facts and information effortlessly.

You will also get to know your brain better and find out how to make it easier to learn and remember information. If you understand how to help your brain work for you, you will be able to unlock your full mental and physical potential.

# The Great Geniuses and Note-making

When you start Mind Mapping, you will be joining the pantheon of great geniuses who all used the major elements of the Mind Map guidelines to make their thoughts visible, and thus to help them and others make great creative leaps forward in their disciplines. These geniuses include:

➡ **Leonardo da Vinci**, voted 'The Brain of the Last Millennium'

➡ **Michelangelo**, the great sculptor and artist

➡ **Charles Darwin**, the great biologist

➡ **Sir Isaac Newton**, discoverer of the laws of gravity

➡ **Albert Einstein**, who discovered the laws of relativity

➡ **Sir Winston Churchill**, the renowned political leader and author

➡ **Pablo Picasso**, who changed the face of 20th-century art

➡ **William Blake**, the English visionary, artist and poet

➡ **Thomas Edison**, the inventor of the light bulb

➡ **Galileo**, who turned the universe inside-out with his astronomical observations

➡ **Thomas Jefferson**, the polymath and architect of the Declaration of Independence

➡ **Richard Feynman**, the Nobel Prize-winning scientist

➡ **Marie Curie**, the double Nobel Prize-winning chemist and radiologist

➡ **Martha Graham**, the great dancer and choreographer

➡ **Ted Hughes**, the late English Poet Laureate, regularly praised as one of the greatest poets of the 20th century

You are in good company! Indeed, it is thought by many that the entire Italian Renaissance was generated for the most part by great creative geniuses who escaped from their linear-thinking prisons. They made their thoughts and ideas visible, not only through lines and words, but also with the equally and often more powerful language of images, drawings, diagrams, codes, symbols, and graphs.

# THE BEST WAY TO MAKE THOUGHTS VISIBLE

The reason why these great creative geniuses used a powerful language of images to organize, develop, and remember their thoughts is because the brain has a natural aptitude for visual recognition – it is, in fact, practically perfect. This is why you are much more likely to remember information when you use images to represent it.

There have been many studies to prove this. For example, in one study adults were shown 2,560 photographic slides at the rate of one every 10 seconds. They were then shown 280 pairs of slides, one of which they had already seen, the other of which they had not. The adults had an 85–95 per cent success rate of correctly identifying the slides they had already seen.

Mind Maps use your brain's talent for visual recognition to great effect. With their combination of colour, image, and curving branches, they are much more visually stimulating than conventional note-taking methods, which tend to be linear and monochrome. This makes it extremely easy to recall information from a Mind Map.

# Mind Mappers in History

## LEONARDO DA VINCI

For a perfect example of a great creative genius using the language of vision to generate thousands of brilliant groundbreaking ideas, you just have to take a look at the notebooks of Leonardo da Vinci. Leonardo used images, diagrams, symbols, and illustrations as the purest way to capture, on paper, the thoughts that were teeming in his brain. At the heart of Leonardo's notebooks, which, because of the manifestations of the sheer creative genius that they contain, are among the most valuable books in the world, are his drawings. These drawings helped Leonardo to explore his thinking in fields as far ranging as art, physiology, engineering, aquanautics, and biology.

For Leonardo the language of words took second place to the language of images, and was used to label, indicate, or describe his creative thoughts and discoveries – the prime tool for his creative thinking was the language of images.

## GALILEO GALILEI

Galileo was another of the world's great creative-thinking geniuses, who, in the late 16th and early 17th centuries, helped to revolutionize science by using his own note-taking techniques. While his contemporaries were using traditional verbal and mathematical approaches to the analysis of scientific problems, Galileo made his thoughts visible, like Leonardo, with illustrations and diagrams.

Interestingly, Galileo was, like Leonardo, a great daydreamer. According to the now famous 'Legend of the Lamp', Galileo was idly watching the gentle swaying to-and-fro of the lamps hanging in Pisa Cathedral when he had a 'Eureka' experience. Galileo realized that no matter what the range of a lamp's swing, it always required the same time to complete an oscillation. Galileo developed this observation of 'isochronism' into his Law of the Pendulum, applying it to timekeeping and the development of the pendulum clock.

# RICHARD FEYNMAN

Richard Feynman, the Nobel Prize-winning physicist, realized as a young man that imagination and visualization were the most vital part of the creative-thinking process. As such he played imagination games, and taught himself to draw.

Like Galileo, Feynman broke away from his more traditional note-taking contemporaries, and decided to put the entire theory of quantum electrodynamics into freshly visual and diagrammatic form. This led to his developing the now famous Feynman diagrams – pictorial representation of particle interaction, which are now used throughout the world by students to help them understand, remember, and create ideas in the realms of physics and general science.

Feynman was so proud of his diagrams that he painted them on his car!

# ALBERT EINSTEIN

Albert Einstein, the brain of the 20th century, also rejected the traditional standard linear, numerical, and verbal forms of creative thinking. Like Leonardo and Galileo before him, Einstein believed that these tools were useful but not necessary, and that imagination was far more important.

Einstein stated that: *'Imagination is more important than knowledge, for imagination is limitless.'* Indeed, in a letter to his friend Maurice Solovine, he explained his difficulty in using words to express his philosophy of science, because he did not think in such ways; he thought more diagrammatically and schematically.

To start your exploration, imagine that your brain is a newly built and empty library waiting to be filled with data and information in the form of books, videos, films, CDs, and DVDs.

You are the chief librarian and have to choose first whether you wish to have a small or a large selection. You naturally choose a large selection.

Your second choice is whether to have the information organized or not. Imagine that you take the second option, *not* to have it organized: you simply order a cartload of books and electronic media, and have it all piled in a giant heap of information in the middle of your library floor!

When somebody comes into your library and asks for a specific book or place where they can find information on a specific topic, you shrug your shoulders and say: 'It's somewhere there in the pile, hope you find it – good luck!'

This metaphor describes the state of most people's minds. Their minds, even though they may – and often do – contain the information they want, are so horribly disorganized that it is impossible for them to retrieve that information when they need it. This leads to frustration and a reluctance to take in or handle any new information. After all, what is the point of taking in new information, if you are never going to be able to access the stuff anyway?!

Imagine, on the other hand, that you have a giant library, filled with incredible amounts of information on everything you ever wanted to know. In this new super-library, rather than all this information being piled randomly in the middle of the floor, everything is filed in perfect order, exactly where you want it.

In addition to this, the library has a phenomenal data-retrieval and access system that enables you to find anything you want at the flash of a thought.

**An impossible dream?**

**An immediate possibility for you!**

Mind Maps **are** that phenomenal storage, data-retrieval, and access system for the gigantic library that actually exists in your amazing brain.

 **Mind Maps help you to learn, organize, and store as much information as you want, and to classify it in natural ways that give you easy and instant access (perfect memory) to whatever you want.**

Mind Maps have an additional strength: you would think that the more information you put into your head, the more stuffed your head would become and the more difficult it would be to get any information out. Mind Maps turn this thought on its head!

*How?*

With Mind Maps each new piece of information you put into your library automatically 'hooks on to' all the information already in there. With more of these grappling hooks of memory attaching to any piece of information in your head, the more easy it is for you to 'hook out' whatever information you need. With Mind Maps, the more you know and learn, the easier it is to learn and know more!

In summary, Mind Mapping has a whole range of advantages that help make your life easier and more successful.

It's time for you to start your first one!

# What Do You Need to Make a Mind Map?

Because Mind Maps are so easy to do and so natural, the ingredients for your 'Mind Map Recipe' are very few:

→ Blank unlined paper

→ Coloured pens and pencils

→ Your brain

→ Your imagination!

# 7 Steps to Making a Mind Map

1. Start in the CENTRE of a blank page turned sideways. Why? **Because starting in the centre gives your brain freedom to spread out in all directions and to express itself more freely and naturally.**

2. Use an IMAGE or PICTURE for your central idea. Why? **Because an image *is* worth a thousand words and helps you use your Imagination. A central image is more interesting, keeps you focussed, helps you concentrate, and gives your brain more of a buzz!**

3. Use COLOURS throughout. Why? **Because colours are as exciting to your brain as are images. Colour adds extra vibrancy and life to your Mind Map, adds tremendous energy to your Creative Thinking, and is fun!**

4. CONNECT your MAIN BRANCHES to the central image and connect your second- and third-level branches to the first and second levels, etc. Why? **Because your brain works by *association*. It likes to link two (or three, or four) things together. If you connect the branches, you will understand and remember a lot more easily.** Connecting your main branches also creates and establishes a basic structure or architecture for your thoughts. This is very similar to the way in which in nature a tree has connected branches that radiate from its central trunk. If there were little gaps between the trunk and its main branches or between those main branches and the smaller branches and twigs, nature wouldn't work quite so well! Without connection in your Mind Map, everything (especially your memory and learning!) falls apart. Connect!

5. Make your branches CURVED rather than straight-lined. Why? **Because having nothing but straight lines is *boring* to your brain.** Curved, organic branches, like the branches of trees, are far more attractive and riveting to your eye.

6. Use ONE KEY WORD PER LINE. Why? **Because single key words give your Mind Map more power and flexibility.** Each single word or image is like a multiplier, generating its own special array of associations and connections. When you use single key words, each one is freer and therefore better able to spark off new ideas and new thoughts. Phrases or sentences tend to dampen this triggering effect. A Mind Map with more key words in it is like a hand with all the finger joints working. A Mind Map with phrases or sentences is like a hand with all your fingers held in rigid splints!

7. Use IMAGES throughout. Why? **Because each image, like the central image, is also worth a thousand words.** So if you have only 10 images in your Mind Map, it's already the equal of 10,000 words of notes!

# Creating Your First Mind Map

To create your first Mind Map, we are going to take as a topic – your next holiday! You are going to use your powers of imagination and association to make a Mind Map about where you want to go.

## LEVEL ONE

First take a sheet of plain paper and some coloured pens. Turn the piece of paper on its side, so that it is wider than it is long (landscape rather than portrait). In the centre of the page draw an image that sums up holidays for you. Use the coloured pens and be as creative as you like.

Now label this image. This could be the name of your destination or simply along the lines of 'My Holiday.'

**Central idea of your first Mind Map**

# LEVEL TWO

Next, draw some thick branches radiating out from the central holiday image. Use a different colour for each. These branches will represent your main thoughts on what this is going to be. You can add any number of branches when you make a Mind Map, but, for the purposes of this exercise, limit the number of branches to five or six.

On each branch, print clearly and in large capital letters the first five single key words that leap to mind when you think about your next holiday.

If you need to help your imagination choose these key words, ask yourself a few questions, such as 'Where will I be going?' (your key word could be 'DESTINATION'), 'What kind of holiday do I want to take?' (your key word could be 'TYPE'), 'What do I need to take with me?' (your key word could be 'LUGGAGE'), and so on. In this example the key words are 'TYPE,' 'EQUIPMENT,' 'CLOTHES,' 'SHUTDOWN,' 'BUDGET,' and 'BOOKING.'

As you can see, at the moment, your Mind Map is primarily composed of colours, lines, and words. So how can we improve it?

We can make it better by adding to it the important brain ingredients of pictures and images from your *imagination*. 'A picture is worth a thousand words' and therefore saves you a *lot* of time and wasted energy writing down those thousand words in your notes. And it is easier to remember.

As you continue developing your Mind Map, add little pictures to represent your ideas and reinforce it. Use your coloured pens and a little imagination. It doesn't have to be a masterpiece – a Mind Map is not a test of your artistic ability. Make sure that you place your images on the branches of your Mind Map.

**Central image with branches to represent your main thoughts about the holiday**

## LEVEL THREE

Now let's use association to expand this Mind Map to its next stage. Returning to your Mind Map, take a look at the key words you have written down on each of the main branches. Do these key words spark off further ideas? For example, if, say, one of your main ideas is 'Booking' think about the different ways you might book it or when you might book it. Would it be through an agent, the Internet, the library or simply a recommendation from a friend?

Draw further branches radiating from each of your key words in order to accommodate the associations you make. Again, the number of sub-branches you have is totally dependent on the number of ideas you come up with – which may be endless. However, for this exercise, limit yourself to three or four sub-branch levels.

On these sub-branches do exactly the same as you did in the first stage of this game: print, clearly, single key words on these waiting-to-be-filled branches. Use the main word on the branch to trigger your three or four new key words on the next-level branches.

Again, remember to use colour and images on these sub-branches.

Congratulations! You've just completed your first Mind Map. You will notice that even at this early stage your Mind Map is brimming with symbols, codes, lines, words, colours and images, and is already demonstrating all the basic guidelines you need in order to apply your brain most effectively and enjoyably. Even better, when it comes to organizing your next holiday, you'll have everything, on a single sheet of paper, you need to consider.

In the next chapter, you're going to learn a lot more about your amazing brain and its phenomenal potential. The more you understand about your brain, the better you will be able to use it.

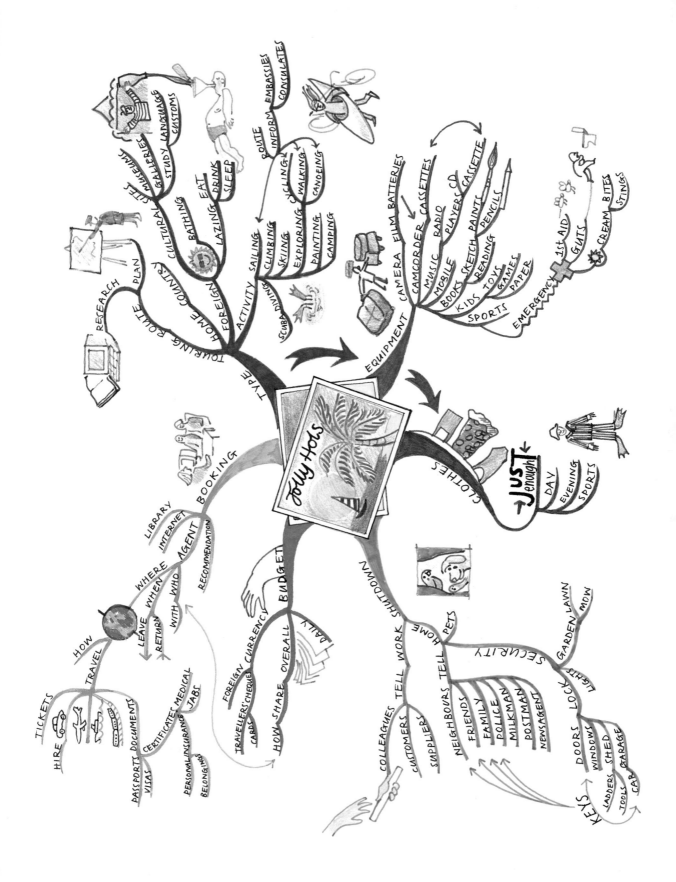

# Mind Maps in Action

 **Millions of people around the world use Mind Maps every day to help them. Some people use them simply to become better planners or more confident public speakers, while others use them to solve problems on a much grander scale.**

## STAND UP AND SPEAK

Mark had always been nervous about addressing large numbers of people in public, but when he was asked to stand up and give a speech at his best friend's wedding he was torn between his anxiety and the pleasure of the invitation.

Normally, he found it difficult to strike a balance between planning and spontaneity: either he lost his train of thought and stumbled over words or he tended to read verbatim from his notes and deliver a monotonous speech.

Mark decided to Mind Map his speech. He brainstormed his ideas with a Mind Map and then structured how he would deliver it on a second Mind Map, exploring the introduction, main themes, and conclusion.

Mark rehearsed it several times using the key words on his second Mind Map. When it came to the big day, he stood up with confidence and delivered the best speech of his life. At least half of the guests approached him afterwards to tell him it was the best speech at a wedding they'd ever heard, too!

# A CITY IN CRISIS

After the terrible events of 9/11 and the collapse of the World Trade Center, the vital utilities to large areas of New York City were thrown into chaos. Communication lines, electricity, water, gas and sewerage networks were in disarray, and residents and businesses were faced with further trauma and hardship.

It was Con Edison, the suppliers of gas and electricity to New York, that had to face the massive challenge of restoring power to the residents of Manhattan. Fortunately, Con Edison had a vital tool to help them: Mind Maps.

Con Edison hosted teams from public utilities in all regions to develop a complex action plan to route their way through the crisis. Together they drew up a mega Mind Map, brainstorming on it all the problems and necessary solutions they faced.

Each step was prioritized and sequenced, and the impact of the failure of one utility on another examined, and this formed the basis of an operations guide. For example, in some cases they would have to re-establish electricity supplies before they could monitor and recommence the movement of water, gas, and sewerage.

Con Edison linked up their Mind Map with a large-screen monitor to provide live-time data displays. The Mind Map included web-links to all key documents. In this way, they could easily disseminate the information to all the different teams involved in the recovery plan. Con Edison resumed their normal utilities service efficiently and, by identifying and documenting the risks faced and the dangers involved, safely.

This meeting of the resources, ideas, and know-how of the various utilities through the medium of Mind Maps minimized the distress experienced by an already traumatized community.

# Know Your Brain, Unlock Your Potential

*The brain regulates all bodily functions; it controls our most primitive behaviour – eating, sleeping, keeping warm; it is responsible for our most sophisticated activities – the creation of civilization, of music, art, science, and language. Our hopes, thoughts, emotions, and personality are all lodged – somewhere – inside there. After thousands of scientists have studied it for centuries, the only word to describe it remains: 'AMAZING'.*

Professor R Ornstein, author of *The Psychology of Consciousness*

# Overview of Chapter 2:

How Well Do You Know Your Brain?

Our Evolving Knowledge of Our Evolving Brains

The 'Left and Right' Brain

The Brain Principle of Synergy

The Learning Principle of Repetition

Knowing about how your brain works can be likened to knowing how to drive a car: the better your knowledge of driving and how to do it, the better at it you will be. If you understand how your brain likes to learn and function, it will reward you by working better for you. You will find it easier to come up with inspired ideas, to remember information when you need it, and to find creative solutions to problems. As you will soon discover, the way you draw a Mind Map reflects the manner in which your brain likes to think. Mind Maps will help you unlock the full potential of your brain. First of all, let's delve into the secrets of your brain. We'll start with a little quiz.

# How Well Do You Know Your Brain?

We use our brains all the time, but how much do we actually know about them? Take a look at the mini brain quiz below to find out how much you know about your personal powerhouse.

## Mini Brain Quiz

1. The number of brain cells in the human brain is:

   a) 100,000?             d) 100,000,000?

   b) 1,000,000?           e) 1,000,000,000?

   c) 10,000,000?          f) 1,000,000,000,000?

2. The brain of an insect like the bee contains millions of brain cells. **True/False?**

3. The 'population' of brain cells in your head is larger than the number of human beings on planet earth. **True/False?**

4.  We have been able to photograph a still picture of a brain cell, but have not yet been able to video a living brain cell. **True/False?**

5.  The great geniuses in history such as Leonardo da Vinci, Isaac Newton, Marie Curie, and Albert Einstein probably reached their maximum potential. **True/False?**

6.  The human brain can grow new connections between brain cells as it ages but cannot generate entirely new cells. **True/False?**

7.  The number of patterns of thought possible for your brain is equal to the number of atoms in:

    a)  A molecule?          e)  The earth?
    b)  A cathedral?         f)  Our solar system including the sun?
    c)  A mountain?          g)  Our galaxy and its 200 billion stars?
    d)  The moon?            h)  None of these?

8.  Your brain is hard-wired – there is not much you can do to change its abilities. **True/False?**

9.  The world's best computers are now better than the human brain in their basic potential. **True/False?**

10. The cerebral cortex is the part of the brain normally referred to as the 'left/right brain'. **True/False?**

11. The right cerebral cortex is the creative side of the brain. **True/False?**

12. The left cerebral cortex is the academic/intellectual side of the brain. **True/False?**

Answers are on p. 65. How many did you get right? Did some of the answers amaze you? Prepare to be even more impressed at how incredible that amazing brain of yours truly is.

# Our Evolving Knowledge of Our Evolving Brains

Although the brain as we know it began evolving some 500 million years ago, the brain's knowledge of the brain has a much, much shorter history. As little as 2,500 years ago humankind knew virtually nothing about the brain and its internal workings. Before the Ancient Greeks, the mind was not even considered to be part of the human body, but was thought to exist as some form of ethereal vapor, gas or disembodied spirit.

Surprisingly, the Greeks did not get us that much further, and even Aristotle – their most famous philosophical thinker and the founder of modern science – concluded that the centre of sensation and memory was located in the heart!

During the Renaissance in the late 14th century, a period of great intellectual awakening, it was finally realized that the centre of thought and consciousness was located in the head, and it was not until the late 20th century that the really great strides forward in our understanding of our own brains were made.

These developments are so significant that they are already changing the foundations of psychology, education, and business, and are emphasizing a fact sensed by many but until now impossible to 'prove' – that the average brain is far more capable than we ever believed!

A number of recent findings stand out as particularly significant.

One of the most important developments is the awareness by the brain of the brain itself. Consider this:

 **95 percent of all that the human race has ever discovered about the internal workings of its own brain has been discovered in the last 10 years!**

What this means is that the human race is at a turning-point in evolution, where we are suddenly discovering amazing facts about our own brains (your brain!): we are beginning to realize that the bio-computer we all have between our ears is infinitely more powerful than we had ever thought.

# Your Brain Cell – a History of Our Knowledge

For centuries the human brain had been considered merely as a three-and-a-half pound structureless, characterless lump of gray matter. And then the intrigue began. With the development of the microscope it was discovered that the brain's crumpled outer layer was far more complex than had previously been suspected. It was found that the brain was composed of thousands of intricate and tiny rivers of blood that coursed throughout it, 'feeding' the brain.

Next came the revolutionary and revelationary discovery that the brain seemed to be composed of hundreds of thousands of tiny dots, the nature and function of which remained a mystery for a while. Then, as the power of the microscope increased, it was found that there were many more 'dots' than previously had been thought, and that each one appeared to have tiny extensions emanating from it. This launched a scientific saga similar to that of astronomy – in which the telescope and its discovery of the stars, solar systems, galaxies and clusters of galaxies was the twin of the microscope and its penetration of the universe of your brain.

As the super-sensitive electron microscope appeared on the scene, scientists observed that each brain was composed of millions of tiny cells, called neurons. The body of each brain cell was found to be astoundingly complex, with a centre, or nucleus, and a large number of branches radiating from it in all directions. The cells looked like beautifully complex trees that had been able to grow branches in all directions round it, and in three dimensions. In fact, if you look at the illustration opposite of the brain cell, you will see that it, not surprisingly,  has the same shape and structure as a Mind Map!

## THE NUMBER OF YOUR BRAIN CELLS

The next stage in this Star Trek-like exploration of the microscopic universe was truly mind-boggling. In the last half of the 20th century, it was discovered that the number of brain cells was not just a few million – it was a million million! 167 times the number of people on the planet!

The significance of this number would be immense, even if each brain cell could perform only very basic operations. If each brain cell were, however, immensely powerful, the significance of their number would take scientists into realms that are almost supernatural.

How powerful are these brain cells? Well, read on ...

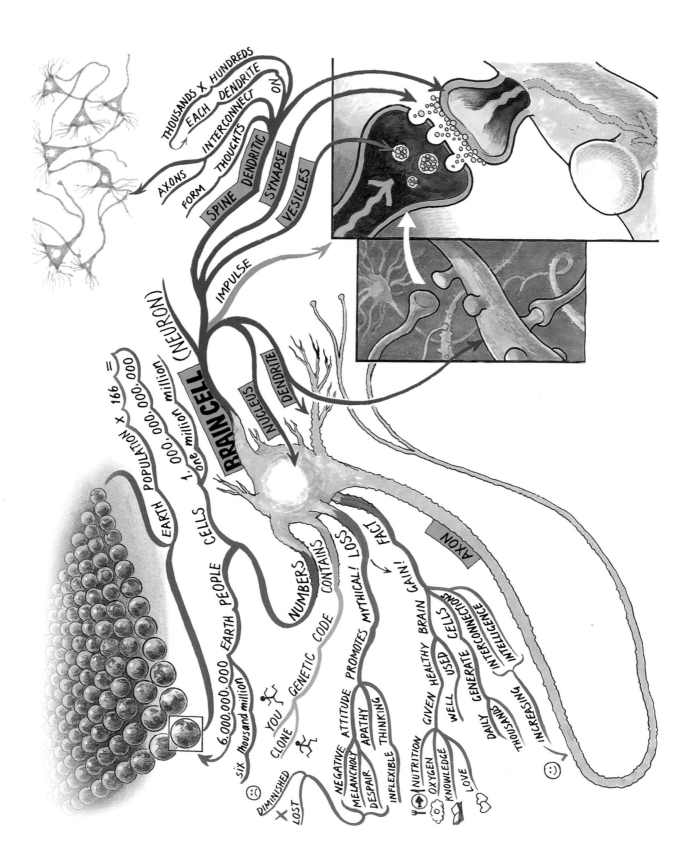

# Brain Cell Power!

Before we consider the power of the human brain cell, let's first analyse the brain capacity of an insect such as a bee. Why? Because, surprisingly, the bee (and every other living animal) has the same super-bio-computer chip as a human. What a bee can do with only a few brain cells puts into sharp relief *your* potential using *millions* of millions of the same brain cells.

## Mind Map exercise: what can a bee do?

Take a large piece of paper and quickly Mind Map all the things you think a bee can do. You could start by drawing a bee as your central image and then add main branches with ideas of the major things you think of, such as 'FLY.' Add sub-branches to these main branches to fully explore each of the main ideas you have.

When you start thinking about it, bees can do the most amazing things with their brains. They can:

1.  **Build**. Bees are among the master architects of the insect world, constructing intricate and complex 'high-rises' that can house entire communities.

2.  **Care** for their young.

3.  **Collect** pollen and information.

4.  **Communicate**. By movement, sound, and gesture, bees can communicate to others intricate information concerning plant locations and types of blossom.

5.  **Count**. Bees can locate chosen objects again by remembering the number of significant items on the way to the desired goal.

6.  **Dance**. When bees return to the hive they perform a complex dance that conveys to their companions the location and navigational information about a new find.

7.  **Distinguish** other bees.

8.  **Eat**.

9.  **Fight**. Not only fight, but fight with such ferocity, focus, speed, and coordination of their multiple fighting appendages, that they make even speeded-up karate films look slow and pathetic by comparison.

10.  **Fly**.

11.  **Hear**. Just like us.

12.  **Learn**. See points 4 and 5 above.

13.   **Live** in an organized community and function appropriately (compare with our own behavior!).

14.   **Make decisions.** Bees can decide to change the temperature of their hive, to convey or not convey information, to fight and to migrate.

15.   **Navigate.** On a miniature scale, the bee is the equivalent of any of our most sophisticated aircraft. Imagine trying to land (which a bee can) on a waving leaf in a strong and gusting wind.

16.   **Produce** honey.

17.   **Regulate** temperature. When the hive becomes too hot, a group of bees will work in harmony to 'reset' the temperature of the hive to within one-tenth of a degree centigrade, using their wings as a giant communal fan, and beating cool air through the hive until the desired temperature is reached.

18.   **Remember.** They could not count, communicate or survive if they didn't!

19.   **Reproduce.**

20.   **See**, including ultraviolet light.

21.   **Smell.**

22.   **Swarm** in more intricate formation than jet fighter squadrons.

23.   **Taste.**

24.   **Think.**

25.   **Touch.**

The Mind Map opposite sums up all the things a bee can do.

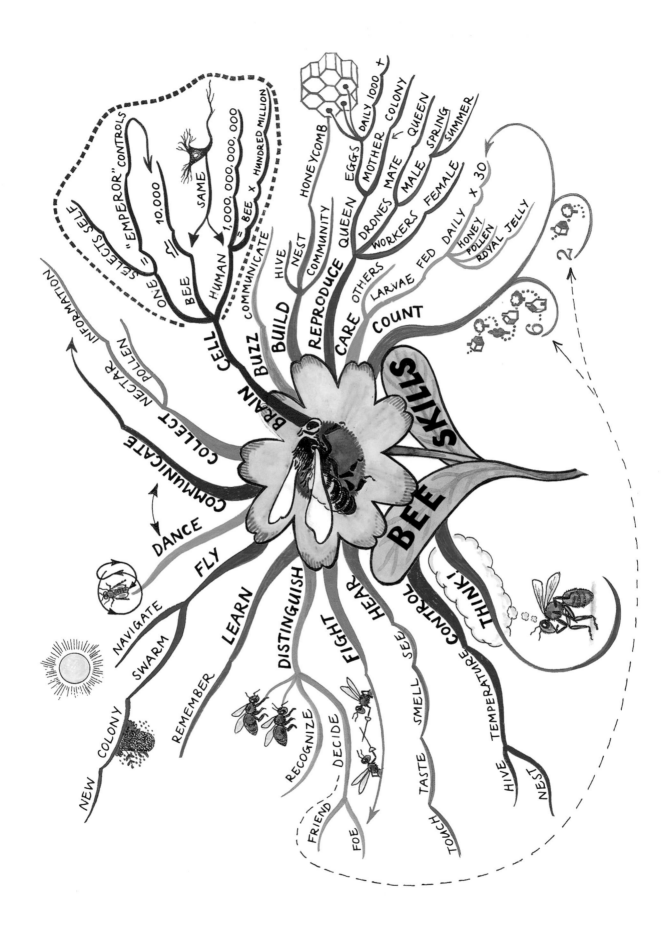

BEE SKILLS

BRAIN

CELL
"EMPEROR" controls
SELECTS SELF
ONE = 10,000
BEE
SAME
HUMAN
1,000,000,000,000
= BEE × HUNDRED MILLION
COMMUNICATE

BUZZ

BUILD
HONEYCOMB
HIVE
NEST
COMMUNITY

REPRODUCE
QUEEN
EGGS DAILY 1000 +
MOTHER COLONY
MATE
DRONES MALE QUEEN
WORKERS MALE SPRING
FEMALE SUMMER
FEMALE

CARE OTHERS
LARVAE FED DAILY × 30
HONEY
POLLEN
ROYAL JELLY

COUNT
2
6

COLLECT
NECTAR
POLLEN
INFORMATION

COMMUNICATE
DANCE

FLY
NAVIGATE
SWARM
NEW COLONY
REMEMBER

LEARN

DISTINGUISH
RECOGNIZE
DECIDE
FRIEND
FOE

FIGHT

HEAR
SEE
SMELL
TASTE
TOUCH

CONTROL
TEMPERATURE
HIVE
NEST

THINK!

BEE

How many brain cells does the bee have in order to do all these things? Millions? No. Fewer than a million. A bee has approximately 960,000 brain cells.

If a bee can do all this with its relatively few thousand brain cells, are we making the most of *our* million, million cells? Probably not!

# The Intricate Structure of Brain Cells

As microscopes became more sophisticated, scientists discovered more and more about our brains. They saw that each cell had its own centre, a nucleus, and that this nucleus was much more than simply 'the centre of the brain cell'. It was, rather, the brain cell's own 'brain' and, based on what we know about the bee, a tiny brain of magnificent power. Literally, a brain within a brain, within your brain!

Then, at the end of the 20th century, another miraculous discovery was made. The Max Planck Laboratory filmed, for the first time in human history, a living brain cell. It had been taken from a living brain and was contained in a deep rectangular channel of brain fluid in a petri dish under the electron-microscope. The film, which has changed the lives of all those who have seen it, showed this amazing little being to have a completely independent intelligence. With its hundreds of baby-like hands, like an amoeba, it extended and retracted, sensitively and focusedly reaching out to every atom of the space in its newly confined universe – looking for **connection** – a moving Mind Map. It was like seeing the most impossibly delicate, sensitive, and intelligent being from outer space. How, then, does each one of these amazing brain-cell creatures relate to others?

# THE BRAIN CELL AND ITS FRIENDS

Your brain cell operates by forming fantastically complex links with tens of thousands of its neighbours and companions. These links are made primarily when its main and biggest branch (the axon) makes multiple thousands of connections with the little buttons on many thousands of many branches of many thousand other brain cells.

Each contact point is known as a synapse. When an electro-magnetic bio-chemical message (the nerve impulse) surges down the axon, it is released through the synaptic button, which is connected to the dendritic spine. Between the two there is a tiny space.

The nerve impulse fires hundreds of thousands of the spheres called vesicles across the synaptic gap in what, in the microcosmic world, must look like a mega Niagara Falls. These vesicles journey at lightning speed across the synaptic gap and attach, like millions of messenger pigeons, to the surface of the dendritic spine. The messages are then transmitted along the branches of the receiving brain cell to its own axon, which then transmits the message through its branches to other brain cells, and so on and on and on, creating the intricate pathway of a thought. These pathways are maps, the internal, physical Mind Maps of your thought. The Mind Maps you make on paper reflect these Mind Maps in your head.

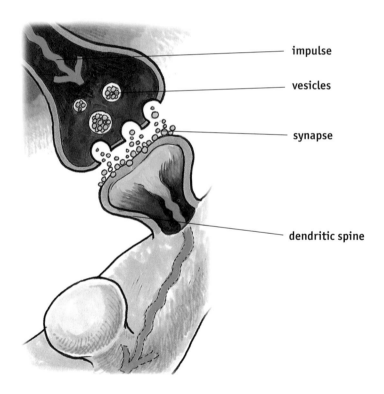

impulse

vesicles

synapse

dendritic spine

A brain cell and its connections

# Just How Powerful Is Your Brain?

If the size of the world's most powerful computer in the year 2000 were represented by the size of a two-storey house, what size building would represent the potential power of your own brain:

a)   A miniature toy house?

b)   A doll's house?

c)   A house the size of a normal room?

d)   An apartment?

e)   A normal two-storey house?

f)   A mansion?

g)   A palace?

h)   A 100-storey skyscraper?

i)   Bigger than all the above?

By now it should be becoming apparent to you that your average brain cell dwarfs the capacity of the average personal computer, and the answer is in fact i) 'bigger than all the above'!

In fact, if we were to represent the strength and power of the world's greatest super-computer by that two-storey house, the potential power of your own brain would be represented by a building far bigger than the 100-storey skyscraper. The strength and power of your own brain would be represented by a heaven-scraper 10 blocks square at the base and reaching to the moon!

# Different Parts, Different Functions

Another key revelation in the history of the brain was our realization that different parts of the brain control different functions.

When the brain started to evolve over 500 million years ago, it developed simultaneously from bottom to top and from back to front.

The different parts of the brain

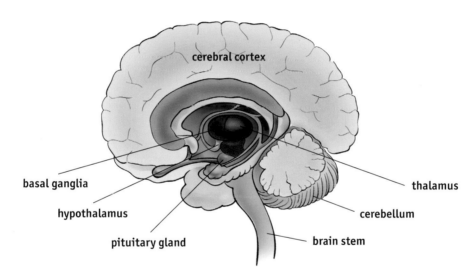

cerebral cortex

basal ganglia

hypothalamus

pituitary gland

thalamus

cerebellum

brain stem

The human brain evolved in the following order:

→ **The brain stem**, which controls life-supporting functions such as breathing and heart rate.

→ **The cerebellum**, or hind brain, which controls movements of the body in space and stores memories for basic learned responses.

→ **The limbic system**, which is slightly more forward in position and includes the thalamus and basal ganglia – the mid-brain. The limbic system is critical for learning and short-term memory but also maintains homeostasis in the body (blood pressure, body temperature, and blood-sugar levels).

→ **The cerebrum**, or cerebral cortex, which covers the rest of the brain and is significantly forward in its position. The cerebrum is the universe's evolutionary masterpiece and is responsible for a vast range of skills including memory, communication, decision making, and creativity. It is the flower of evolution, it is the latest part of the brain to develop, and it is the part that allows us to Mind Map. Mind Mapping is a function of evolution's highest masterpiece.

In the next couple of pages you will follow the history of evolution's development of the brain and our intelligence, culminating in the cerebellum and the brain's ability to Mind Map.

# The Brain Stem

**Evolved:** 500 million years ago.

**Common title:** Reptilian Brain or Primitive Brain.

**Location:** Deep down in the brain, extending up from your spinal cord.

**Functions:** Basic life support. Handles breathing and heart rate. Masterminds general level of alertness. Alerts you to important incoming sensory information. Controls temperature. Controls the digestive process. Relays information from the cerebellum.

**Interesting fact:** Recent research seems to be suggesting that this area of your brain may be far more 'intelligent' than we had previously thought.

Recent studies of the giant reptiles, such as alligators and crocodiles, whose entire brain is basically the brain stem, have shown that they have highly evolved forms of social behaviour, deep family and group relationships, and emotions.

Next time you see one of these giant reptiles, live or on film, look more closely to see the magnificent brain stem in action!

# The Cerebellum

**Evolved:** Approximately 400 million years ago.

**Common title:** Little Brain or Hind Brain.

**Location:** Attached to the rear of the brain stem – part of the lower brain.

**Function:** Controls body position, poise, and balance. Monitors movement in space. Stores memories for basic learned responses. Transmits vital information via the brain stem to the brain.

**Interesting fact:** In the human brain, the cerebellum has more than tripled in size in the last one million years.

# The Limbic System

**Evolved:** Between 300 and 200 million years ago.

**Common title:** Mammalian Brain or Mid-Brain.

**Location:** Between the brain stem and the cortex.

**Function:** Maintains blood pressure, heart rate, body temperature, and blood-sugar levels. Governs navigational skills in the hippocampus. Critical to learning and for short-term and long-term memory, and stores memories of life experiences. Maintains homeostasis (constant environment) in the body. Involved in survival emotions of sexual desire or self-protection.

**Interesting facts:**

1.  Scientist Robert Ornstein says: 'One way to remember limbic functions is that they are the four 'F's of survival: feeding, fighting, fleeing and sexual reproduction.'

2.  The limbic system contains the hypothalamus, often regarded as the most important part of the 'mammalian brain'. It is often known as the 'brain' of the brain. Although tiny (about the size of half a sugar cube) and weighing only four grams, it regulates hormones, sexual desire, emotions, eating, drinking, body temperature, chemical balances, sleeping and waking, while at the same time masterminding the master gland of the brain, the pituitary.

3.  The hippocampus is increasingly thought to be the seat of learning and memory. In shape it looks remarkably like a little seahorse.

Two other major areas of the mid-brain include the thalamus, which makes preliminary classifications of external information reaching the brain, and which relays information to the cortex via the hypothalamus. It is the hypothalamus that is the part of your brain which decides what comes to your attention and what does not – for example, telling you at which moment to notice that the room is getting warmer or that you are getting hungrier!

The basal ganglia, which are located on both sides of the limbic system (as is the cerebellum), are concerned with movement control, especially initiating movements. In the human brain (your brain) these networks have been growing larger and better developed over the last few million years.

# The Cerebrum (Cerebral Cortex)

**Evolved:** Approximately 200 million years ago.

**Common title:** The left and right brain.

**Location:** Fits like a giant 'thinking cap' over the entire brain; extends into the full area of your forehead.

**Functions:** Organization. Memory. Understanding. Communication. Creativity. Mind Mapping! Decision making. Speech. Music. Other specific functions include the full range of the 'left/right brain' cortical skills discussed on pages 52–4.

**Interesting facts:**

1. Your cerebrum is by far the largest part of your brain.

2. The cerebrum is covered by that evolutionarily magical one-eighth-inch thick, amazingly corrugated layer of nerve cells known as the cerebral cortex. It is the nature of our particular cortex that identifies you as human.

3. The two cerebral hemispheres are connected by a fabulously intricate network of nerve fibres called the corpus callosum; these 300 million nerve fibres shuttle information back and forward between the two hemispheres.

# DID YOU KNOW THAT...?

→ Since the beginning of time there have been over 90 billion humans born into this world, each one astoundingly different from all the others?

→ The human brain contains a million million neurons or nerve cells?

→ Brain cells are so tiny that you could fit 100 hundred of them on to a single pinhead?

→ Each of your brain cells is more powerful than a standard personal computer?

→ If you lined up all of your brain cells they could reach to the Moon and back? (The Moon is about 238,710 miles [384,000 km] from the Earth.)

→ The human brain can generate thousands of new brain cells every day?

→ The number of internal 'maps of thought' that the brain is capable of producing is 1 followed by 10.5 million kilometres of standard typewritten zeros?

→ To make a machine that could do everything you could do – to make another you – would cost well over a couple of billion dollars? You are highly valuable!

→ At the same time as you make mental connections in your thoughts you are making physical connections in your brain? You are literally making that incredible brain of yours more complex, more sophisticated, and more powerful with every thought connection. The brain with which you are reading this now is therefore not the same as it was yesterday, and it will not be the same tomorrow!

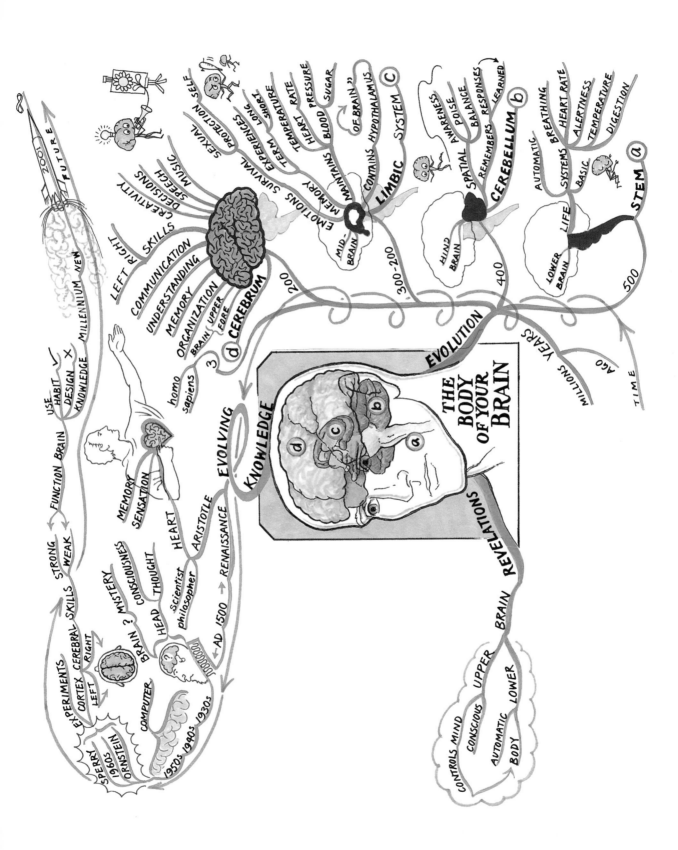

THE BODY OF YOUR BRAIN

EVOLUTION

KNOWLEDGE

REVELATIONS

**d CEREBRUM**

homo sapiens 3
BRAIN UPPER FORE
ORGANIZATION
MEMORY
UNDERSTANDING
COMMUNICATION
SKILLS LEFT RIGHT
CREATIVITY
DECISIONS
SPEECH
MUSIC
SEXUAL PROTECTION
SURVIVAL
EMOTIONS
EXPERIENCES LONG TERM SHORT
MEMORY
MAINTAINS TEMPERATURE HEART RATE BLOOD PRESSURE SUGAR
CONTAINS HYPOTHALAMUS
SELF
"OF BRAIN"
MID-BRAIN

**LIMBIC SYSTEM c**

200
300–200

**CEREBELLUM b**

SPATIAL AWARENESS POISE BALANCE
REMEMBERS RESPONSES LEARNED
HIND BRAIN
400

**STEM a**

AUTOMATIC SYSTEMS
BASIC
BREATHING HEART RATE ALERTNESS TEMPERATURE DIGESTION
LIFE
LOWER BRAIN
500

TIME MILLIONS YEARS AGO

EVOLVING
KNOWLEDGE
MILLENNIUM NEW
USE
HABIT X
DESIGN
KNOWLEDGE
FUNCTION BRAIN
STRONG WEAK
EXPERIMENTS
CEREBRAL SKILLS
CORTEX LEFT RIGHT
BRAIN ? MYSTERY
COMPUTER
SPERRY 1960s ORNSTEIN
1950s 1940s 1930s
AD 1500 → RENAISSANCE
Scientist philosopher
ARISTOTLE
HEART
CONSCIOUSNESS
THOUGHT
HEAD
MEMORY
SENSATION

CONTROLS MIND
CONSCIOUS UPPER
AUTOMATIC LOWER
BODY
BRAIN

2001
FUTURE

# The 'Left and Right' Brain

**The most important area of the brain to understand when it comes to tapping in to your brain power is the cerebrum or, as it is often referred to, the 'left and right' brain.**

This is because the cerebrum controls all the major memory and learning skills that we rely on to make us shine as individuals; if we understand how to tap into the full power of the cerebrum we can strengthen our mental and physical performance in every area of our lives. What do we actually mean by the left and right sides of the brain?

In the 1950s and 1960s Professor Roger Sperry and his team performed some incredible experiments on the cerebral cortex, in conjunction with Professor Robert Ornstein. (Professor Sperry later received the Nobel Prize for his work.) They asked students to perform such varied mental tasks as daydreaming, calculating, reading, drawing, speaking, writing, colouring shapes, and listening to music, while measuring their brainwaves.

The results were a revelation. They observed that, in general, the cerebral cortex divides the tasks into two main categories: left-brained ones and right-brained ones. The right-brain tasks included rhythm, spatial awareness, imagination, daydreaming, colour, dimension, and tasks needing holistic or whole-picture awareness. Left-brained tasks included words, logic, numbers, sequences, lists and analysis.

Left- and right-brain skills

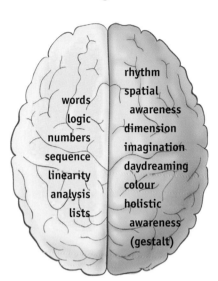

It was also apparent that people who had been trained in skills that relied more on one 'side' their brain than the other went on to form dominant habits that favoured activities controlled by their chosen brain side. What's more, they even described themselves in these terms.

The umbrella terms that evolved in popular parlance were 'academic', 'intellectual', and 'business' for the left-hemispheric activities, and 'artistic', 'creative', and 'intuitive' for the right-hemispheric activities. But these only gave part of the story.

Further research revealed that the ongoing strength and weakness of the cortical skills in any one individual was more a function of habit than of basic brain design. When people who were weak in one area were trained in that area by experts, they invariably increased their skill and strength in that given area, and, what's more, simultaneously strengthened their performance in other areas! For example, if someone who had been weak in drawing skills was trained to draw and paint, their academic performance increased overall, especially in subjects such as geometry where perception and imagination are so important.

Another example is the right-brain skill of daydreaming, which is essential to your brain's survival. Daydreaming gives needed rest to those parts of your brain which have been doing more analytical and repetitious work, exercises your projective and imaginative thinking, and gives you a necessary chance to integrate and create. Most of the great geniuses used directed daydreaming to help them solve problems, generate ideas, and achieve their great goals.

My own work in the fields of creativity, memory, and Mind Mapping has led to identical conclusions. It has shown that by combining the elements of the two hemispheres, it is possible to achieve surprisingly huge increments in overall performance.

Unfortunately, modern educational systems have had a tendency to favour 'left brain' skills – mathematics, languages, and the sciences – over the arts, music, and the teaching of thinking skills, especially creative-thinking skills. In focussing on only half of the brain's skills, you would think that our education systems are, literally, creating half-wits. Unfortunately, the truth of the matter is even worse: a more accurate measure would be 1-percent wits! This is because the brain works on two important principles: **synergy** and **repetition**.

**If you rely heavily on one side of the brain and neglect the other, you drastically reduce the overall potential of your brain.**

Let's take a closer look at why.

# The Brain Principle of Synergy

We used to think that our thinking processes were organized on a simple, additive mathematical principle, whereby every time we added a single new piece of data or new thought into our brain, it simply added one more item to the store.

However, in the second half of the 20th century, we discovered that this was not the case; in fact, the brain operates synergetically. In a synergetic system the whole is greater than the sum of its parts; in other words 1 + 1 will equal more than 2. In such a system, 'more' can reach infinity.

## HOW CAN THIS BE SO?

A simple example from everyday human activity illustrates this well, namely daydreaming. When you are daydreaming (which everyone does, every day) you are engaging not in additive-thinking behaviour, but in multiplying, synergetic thinking.

For example, you take yourself ('one') and someone else (another 'one') and you start to multiply your thoughts. Depending on the other 'one' of your choice, you can daydream about yourself and that other 'one' all day, all week, all month, all year, or, as some people do, all your lifetime! You can use the infinite theatre of your imagination, and its infinite props, to create the most macabre and spine-chilling horror stories and tragedies, or the most glorious and uplifting comedies, romances, fairytales, and epics. The productions of Hitchcock and Spielberg have nothing on your imagination.

In fact, the potential for the human brain (your brain) to generate Mind Maps of thought is, theoretically, infinite.

# You Are the Architect of Yourself

Knowing that your brain thinks synergetically will change the way you think – the way you think about thinking, the way you think about yourself, and the way you think about others – for ever! What it means is that your brain is self-creating. Every thought you think is unique to you, and fits into a network of other thoughts and associations that has never existed before and will never exist again, except in your own brain. Your thought then multiplies into the vast Internet and internal super-Mind Map of your growing memories, fantasies, attitudes and dreams. You are entirely and infinitely unique!

This news is made even more exciting if you realize that as you create more and more positive galaxies and universes of thought, at the same time you are forging new physical connections within your brain. You are literally making your super-bio-computer of a brain and its internal Mind Maps more complex, more sophisticated, more powerful and more successful!

 **You are the engineer and architect of your own physical brain, and the universes of thought that reside within it. Mind Maps help you become, like Leonardo da Vinci, a master engineer.**

# The Learning Principle of Repetition

If the brain works synergetically, how does this influence our capacity to learn? Well, if, for example, 'X' equals memory, then the more appropriately and well you practise using your memory, the more physical connections you will make within your brain, and the easier memorization will become. If 'X' equals creativity, then the more appropriately you practise being creative, the more you will create and the easier creative thinking will become. The more your body is used well, the more successful become its performances. The same principle applies to learning, and to the development of all mental and physical skills. To make the Mind Maps of thought in your head stronger, repetition is an essential thinking tool.

## NEW THOUGHT ABOUT THOUGHT AND NEW THOUGHT

Imagine that you have to cut a complex route or pathway through a patch of virgin jungle, from one side to the other. The first time you go through (the first time you have that thought) there would be lots of resistance to your passage. If, the minute you had reached the other side, you were lifted up by helicopter and placed once again at the starting point, and asked to go through the jungle again, you would encounter, what? Obviously slightly less resistance, because of the pathway you had already made. Every time you went through, you would make the pathway a little larger, and the resistance to your passageway would be a little less each time. If you and others continued to use the pathway, it would eventually become a winding track, then a small road, then a larger road, and eventually a major highway network.

This means that the more you use your brain to think about something, the easier it is to think about it. This is because the biochemical resistance to that particular thought is reduced. In repeating a thought pattern you are more clearly defining the map of that thought in your mind.

Knowing that repetition of a thought reduces resistance will transform your understanding of your behaviour, learning, habits, and the general development of your potential. Why is this?

# PROBABILITIES OF THOUGHTS

If repetition of a thought reduces resistance, then that same repetition must increase the probability of something in turn. The probability of what?! Quickly jot down your thought/s.

The most common responses to this question are:

→ Memory

→ Learning

→ Success

→ Improvement

→ Creativity

→ Intelligence

→ Growth

→ Mental power

The response to each of those answers is 'maybe', 'maybe', 'maybe', 'maybe', …

**Try this:** what does practice make? ...

'Perfect!' is the usual reply.

But does practice make perfect? Supposing you practise the wrong thing? There is one thing that the repetition of a thought increases: it will strengthen the Mind Maps of thought; it will increase the probability of

## REPETITION!

Everything you do or say or think or feel increases the probability that you will do, say, think, or feel in the same way again. If you do things well, speak and think positively, and generally feel good about yourself, others, the world and the universe, the probability continually increases that you will do better, talk and think better, and feel and be better.

# Infinitely Positive or Infinitely Negative?

However (and herein is concealed the lurking mental monster), if you do poorly, think and act negatively, practise inadequately, and regularly feel bad about yourself, others, the world, and the universe, then with every such thought and act you increase the probability of a continuing and deepening downward spiral.

Let's look at a little slogan from the world of artificial intelligence: GIGO. GIGO is computer-speak for 'Garbage In, Garbage Out'! You put garbage into your computer, you get garbage out of it ...

For many years this was also thought to be true for the human brain. We (and you!) now know that this is not so, because of the Synergy Principle. In the case of the human brain it must be: GIGG.

## GARBAGE IN, GARBAGE GROWS!

How far can this garbage grow? Infinitely! Potentially infinite universes of garbage and rubbish are possible! Because of the brain principles of synergy and repetition, our brains can be both infinitely creative and infinitely destructive! The power to use your brain positively and to the greatest effect lies in your hands. Nonetheless, this book will equip you with all the tools to help you harness this power.

## How Many Thoughts Can You Think?

The only limiting factor, biologically, to the number of thoughts, memories, behaviour patterns, and habits that are available to you must lie in the physical limitation of the pattern-making potential of your amazing brain.

With a million, million brain cells, many with hundreds of thousands of branches, each branch with hundreds of thousands of connection points, each with trillions of messengers, and each connection point capable of forming billions upon billions of different patterns, the number must be gigantic.

In fact, the number, as calculated by the then top brain scientist in Russia, Professor Anokhin, is one followed by ten-and-a-half-million kilometres of standard type-written zeros! **This would cover a piece of paper long enough to go to the moon and back 14 times!**

**Professor Anokhin declared that the fundamental potential of the human brain was … infinite! Professor Anokhin's calculation confirms that your brain has the possibility of making a virtually infinite number of Mind Maps.**

Before you read any further, take a look at the Mind Map opposite to help you remember the key principles of synergy and repetition and how they affect the way we think and grow.

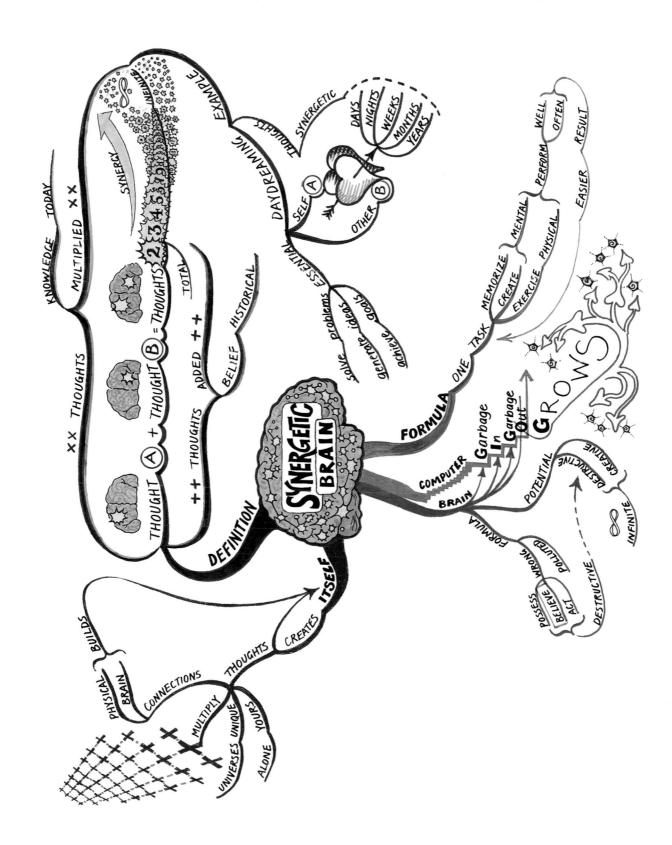

Now that you know how significant these two brain principles are, let's return to the dangers of relying too heavily on either one of the hemispheres of your brain.

**The way that the left and right sides of your cerebral cortex shuttle messages backward and forward between the two hemispheres of the brain creates a synergetic formula for thinking and growth. If you rely too heavily on tasks that challenge only one side of your brain you will discourage the dialogue between the two hemispheres and drastically reduce the overall performance of your brain. In short you will restrict your brain's synergetic way of thinking.**

Also, because the more you repeat a pattern of thinking or behavior the easier it is for your brain to think in that way again, if you always favour left-, or right-brain-associated tasks, you will reinforce that dominance. This means that you will become stuck in a particular pattern of thinking and you will find it much more difficult to tap in to your full potential.

How can you make sure that this doesn't happen? How can you engage both sides of your brain as equally as possible to help unlock your full brain potential? One of the simplest ways to do this is by using Mind Maps to develop your thinking power.

# Mind Maps: Brain Tool Extraordinaire

Why is a Mind Map such a powerful brain-friendly tool? Mind Maps engage **both** sides of the brain because they use image, colour, and imagination (realms of the right brain) in combination with words, number, and logic (realms of the left brain).

How you draw a Mind Map also encourages **synergetic** thinking. Look back at the Mind Map you drew in the previous chapter. The way the branches grow outwards to form another level of sub-branches encourages you to create more ideas out of each thought you add to your Mind Map.

Also, because all the ideas on a Mind Map are linked to each other, it helps your brain to make great leaps of understanding and imagination by **association**. If you had just drawn up a simple list of ideas about your holiday, it is highly unlikely that you would have come up with the same amount of ideas as you did on your Mind Map. This is because the information on your list would not have been linked in a logical or organized way and this would have stifled your brain s synergetic way of thinking.

Whenever you are wanting to plan something, organize your thoughts, brainstorm/brainbloom an idea or unlock your imagination, always draw a Mind Map to develop your ideas. Mind Maps are the thinking tool to unlock your brain power: they reflect the internal Mind Maps of your brain.

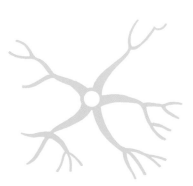

The more you use Mind Maps in your daily life, the easier it becomes to engage both sides of your brain – remember, the more you *repeat* something, the easier it becomes. Mind Maps help you reinforce the maps of thought in your brain. Indeed, you should think of them as an externalization of the thoughts in your head: in drawing a Mind Map of your thoughts, you repeat and reinforce the map of that thought in your mind. Because the structure of a Mind Map resembles the shape of your thought patterns, the act of drawing them is a natural and memorable repetition.

Now that you know how to unlock your brain's potential, it's time to take a look at how you can use Mind Maps in combination with a foolproof success formula so you can succeed in life again and again and again.

## Answers to Mini Brain Quiz

1. **f)**

2. **False** – they contain only a few thousand

3. **True**

4. **False**

5. **False**

6. **False**

7. **h)** – it is far greater than any of the previous possible answers!

8. **False**

9. **False**

10. **True**

11. **True**

12. **True**

# The Ultimate Success Formula

*If you want to succeed, double your failure rate.*

Thomas Watson

# Overview of Chapter 3:

Learning How to Learn

Failure – the Global Reactions

The Success Formula – TEFCAS

The Principle of Persistence

Mind Maps and TEFCAS

This chapter will introduce you to a process of establishing successful Mind Map thinking patterns to make sure your internal Mind Maps of thought get better and better. In the course of the chapter I will introduce you to two new Brain Principles, one of which is the essence of the formula itself, the second of which will help you improve your stamina and staying power.

The focus of this chapter is you as a learning individual: you will learn that the most important of all learning skills is Learning How to Learn.

## Quick brain-check – failure quiz!

1.  Have you ever, in your academic, physical, personal, social, professional, or spiritual lives, had a really good failure? **Yes/No?**

2.  Have you had more than one? **Yes/No?**

3.  Have you ever made the same big mistake twice? **Yes/No?**

You will be pleased to know that everyone answers 'Yes' to all those questions!

The secret of the Learning How to Learn Formula is beginning to emerge ...

# Learning How to Learn – the Ultimate Goal

In any learning situation, whether it be learning a sport, learning to play a musical instrument, learning communication skills, or learning mathematics, there are certain variables that are common to all. These include:

1.  The degree of your success.

2.  The time you have to learn and practise.

3.  The number of times you actually do practise or study. (These are called your 'Learning Trials' – it is useful to think of them as 'try-als' because they are the number of times you try, practise, and study in your learning progress.)

4.  The underlying goal of all learning. Whether you are on your 2nd trial, your 22nd trial, or your 2,002nd trial, what is the underlying goal?

Jot down what you think is this 'goal of goals'. In other words, as you start your next trial, as you are creating new Mind Map thought patterns, what should you be trying to do?

For 30 years I have asked this question of hundreds of thousands of students from all over the world.

The result is amazing. No matter what the person's age, sex, race, country of origin, educational level or primary language, the answer is basically unanimous:

'To get better with every trial'.

Do you agree with the rest of the world, or are you going to establish yourself as a maverick?!

If you chose the route of the maverick, you were correct! The horrifying truth of the matter is that 'to get better with every trial' is not only the wrong formula; it is an extremely dangerous one, concealing the seeds of a self-destructive synergy and an incipient Meta-Negative Thinking Habit. Over 99 percent of the world's population is using a wrong and destructive formula for every learning situation!

I will state categorically that no one has ever been able to apply this wrong formula successfully. No one ever can do or will do.

What then, is the correct formula? Let's explore ...

Below you will find a graph which plots success rate versus the number of learning trials (try-als) over time. Sweeping up from the zero-point is a typical average learning curve. This is the Holy Grail of learning that 99 percent of the world's population tries to emulate.

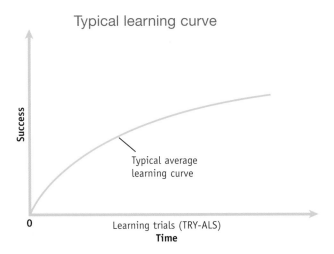

Typical learning curve

Success

Typical average
learning curve

0    Learning trials (TRY-ALS)
Time

What's the problem with this graph? The very fact that this is an average curve. An average curve is the summated norm of all the individual curves. However, each individual curve is precisely that – individual and unique. It will have its own special pattern, and will tend to look very little like the curve in this graph. Let's see what really happens.

Let's imagine that you start learning something at which you are quite confident. You start learning and discover you are reasonably competent. You try and try, passing trial number 25, continue trying and trying up through trial 27, and you are still doing better than average – ahead of the curve. On trial 27 you have a minor, minor setback, but you are tough-minded so you can handle that. On and on you try, progressing and progressing through trial 30 ... 40 ... 50 ... 60 ... 70 ... 80 ... 90, and all is still going well on trials 91, 92, 93, 94, 95 ...

Trial 96 is represented by the giant black hole in the graph below.

Graph representing the giant astronomical Black Hole
of Learning – a Trial that is a complete 'FAILURE'

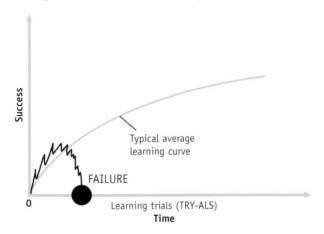

This black ball represents the giant astronomical black hole of learning – FAILURE! This is the kind of situation where you have completely blown a vital examination, have a quintuple bogie on the final hole of a golf tournament you were winning, get knocked out in the first round, totally mess up a relationship you treasured, and break all your New Year's resolutions in one go!

Does everybody have such 'failures?' Of course they do. Does everyone have more than one such failure in their life? Of course they do. Does everyone at some time make the same mistake twice? Of course they do!

# Verbal Responses to Failure

Most people's verbal responses to these 'failure' situations are identical. They are of two major classes. The first of these is of the 'Oh ****!!' type (fill in your own favourites!). The second category is rather more serious, and is the personal 'I *****!' The blanks here are singularly negative:

I:

'Quit'
'Give up'
'Can't'
'Won't'
'Don't care'
'Am a loser'
'Never should have tried this'
'Have no talent for this'
'Will never succeed'
'Didn't want to do it anyway'

These reactions to 'failure' are globally pervasive. They also are the expression of deep-felt emotions that surround the experience of failure. It is these reactions that reinforce the wrong Mind Map patterns in your head.

# Failure – the Global Reactions

Eight of the most common reaction-to-failure words I have heard are listed below. They are unremittingly negative.

If we examine them, we will see that they provide even more invidious poison to your thinking system than might have at first seemed apparent:

**DISGRACED**. Dis-graced. This means that failure takes your grace away. Remember, by feeling so, you make it so.

**UNDIGNIFIED**. Un-dignified. Not only your grace, but your dignity is also removed.

**DIMINISHED**. Made less, smaller, and weaker than you were.

**SHAMEFUL**. Shame-ful. Full of shame. This affirmation leaves no room for anything else.

**DISILLUSIONED**. Dis-illusioned. Your illusion, your vision, has been taken away.

**DEBILITATED**. De-bilitated. Your ability has been similarly removed.

**DISCOURAGED**. Dis-couraged. Your courage has been sucked out, leaving you timid and afraid.

**DEMOTIVATED**. De-motivated. Your motivation is your life force; the energy that enables you to act. 'Failure' makes you sacrifice it.

The snake-pit of this Meta-Negative Thinking produces an overriding and overwhelming *fear*. And what is the underlying fear? The fear of *failure* – the fear of failure at school; the fear of failure in love; the fear of failure at work; the fear of failure in life; and the fear of life itself!

This fear is the main cause of stress. And stress is the cause of a staggering 80 percent of disease.

Faced with such negativity and the actual pain of failure, is it logical for our learning friend to quit? Yes! In the context of a learning goal which says that you must get better with every trial, what is the point of carrying on when you have tried 95 times, only to fail abysmally at the 96th hurdle?

Individuals in this situation often will give up, and will search for some other area of activity where they can pursue the goal of 'getting better with every trial' more successfully. At some point they will inevitably hit the big black hole of failure in this area as well, and will conclude that this activity is not for them either. And on and on they will go, searching for an impossible dream.

The dream is impossible because the human brain is not designed to get better with every trial!

The brain is designed on a far more realistic, experimental, explorative and exciting model:

# The Success Formula – TEFCAS

When you understand **TEFCAS**, you will understand the true nature of learning, and the proper nature of 'failure'; you will have the correct formula for accelerating your own successes. **TEFCAS** is an acronym made up of the first letters of the six major words that define the fundamental steps your brain has to take while learning anything. It is establishing successful new Mind Map thought patterns, i.e. learning:

**T**rial
**E**vent
**F**eedback
**C**heck
**A**djust
**S**uccess

**TEFCAS** is more physics than psychology. It traces, step-by-step, what steps your brain is obliged to take while learning in the physical universe; the laws of which it must both follow and use to its advantage.

**TEFCAS** can be considered your brain's application and adaptation of the Scientific Method. The Scientific Method for thinking is the method for improving your internal Mind Map thought structures – it is the basis of all the great discoveries in science, and is very similar to normal child's play! In the Scientific Method you start with a question or hypothesis. Through a series of investigations you observe the feedback you receive from your actions. You then check the results against the original question or hypothesis, and conclusions are drawn which either confirm or contradict the hypothesis, or satisfy or do not satisfy the question. On the basis of this, the scientist/child then adjusts his or her actions to the ongoing pursuit of knowledge (success), and tries again.

Let's examine each of the six main steps of **TEFCAS**:

# T – TRIAL

No matter what you are learning, nothing will happen if you don't first try. Your learning progress is marked by your number of try-als. When you are learning to juggle you must first throw the ball; when you are learning to dance you must take the first step; when you are learning mathematics you must attempt to derive a new formula; when you are learning to write you must make the first mark. When you have tried, there will inevitably be an:

# E – EVENT

In juggling, the event may be that the ball lands on the floor, or lands on your head, or lands in your hand, or lands in your colleague's coffee cup! The universe does not really care. If you try there will always be an event. This event will inevitably give you:

# F – FEEDBACK

Whether you wish it to or not, the universe supplies you with a cascade of information about your trial and event that feeds back through all your senses. This is one reason why it is so important to have a healthy mind in a healthy body – so that your senses can provide you with more and more pure information. Your brain will absorb this feedback on both the conscious and para-conscious levels. In the juggling example this will include the sight, sound and feeling of the juggling balls. It may also include feedback from your colleague if your ball lands in his or her coffee cup! With all this feedback pouring in, your brain will:

# C – CHECK

This will happen both automatically and consciously, and will be done in relation to your goals. Continuing with the juggling example: your brain will check the energy put into the attempt; its appropriateness; the height and trajectory of the ball in relation to the goal; your breathing; and your poise and posture, etc. Having done this your brain will:

# A – ADJUST

You will compare your performance against your goal, and make what you consider to be appropriate realignments for the next trial. While considering the element of adjustment, you should always consider the underlying goal. No matter what you are learning, the vision toward which you are aiming your efforts is one of:

# S – SUCCESS

No matter what you do, your brain's aim is to succeed in doing it. From tasks as simple as making yourself a cup of tea, to the far more complex and large life-goals, success is the main beacon. At first glance it would appear that the **TEFCAS** formula has no possible room for error. There is, however, a prime danger. The danger lies in the nature of your goal. If I have a negative goal – such as kicking you, or in some other way harming you – I still wish to be successful. In this case my warped view of success will probably lead to a feedback situation that is not to my advantage!

It is therefore essential that your goals in **TEFCAS** be toward a positive success. This is an exact reflection of Meta-Positive Thinking (more on this in the next chapter).

# DID YOU KNOW THAT...?

**There is always more failure than success in a thriving economy?**

This is because all success is the result of failure – before you succeed you need to try again and again until you get it right. If as a child you had given up learning how to walk each time you tried and then failed to walk, you'd still be sitting on your butt! Success is of course the ideal outcome of a trial but it is impossible to find success without a process of learning from each failure.

Society is able to make progress because we fail and fail again – and then succeed. Each success contributes to the overall intellectual capital of a society. This is why a society that encourages failure by default encourages success.

The greatest obstacle to progress and success is a fear of failure. Any system or person that punishes failure discourages the people connected to it from making new attempts. Ironically, the person who so fears failure that they dare not fail will end up being a failure.

According to Dr Adrian Atkinson, a business psychologist and the managing director of Human Factors International, most entrepreneurs fail an average of five times before they are finally successful. He also observes that entrepreneurs regard failure as key learning experiences that lead them to success.

# Learning from Every Little Error Leads to Greater Success

Microsoft is an ongoing success story in the business world. Bill Gates, Microsoft's chairman and chief software architect, loves innovation, is an inspirational leader, and has built up an enviable corporate culture which often sees Microsoft scoring high in surveys dedicated to revealing the best and most productive workplaces around the world.

What has driven Microsoft's success over the years is an inherent ability to look at a piece of software through objective eyes and recognize its failings as well as its strengths. Bill Gates, addressing an audience in the US when launching Microsoft's latest software innovations, referred to a past challenge which faced the company and how Microsoft dealt with it:

*'If anything proves our willingness to listen to our customers and improve, it's the evolution of Word over the years. No doubt that first version was a little clunky, a little bit too much of a technologist's dream. We listened hard. People asked us to change it, and we drove it forward.'*

Gates' attitude to the flaws in his software and his ongoing drive to 'check' and 'adjust' help explain why Gates is such an inspirational – and successful – person.

# TEFCAS and Mind Maps in Action

In 1999 the World Trade Organization annual conference in Seattle made headline news for all the wrong reasons: it attracted strong anti-globalization protests that led to many arrests, US$3 million of damage, and business losses of more than US$10 million. Protest and disruption became familiar themes at ensuing conferences in following years, though not on such a wide scale.

In November 2003 Mexico was to host the annual conference in Cancun. Protesters promised disruption on a grander scale than Seattle. The Mexican government and military, in conjunction with the Mexican security company Vitalis, decided to Mind Map all the possible disruption that could take place during the conference week. They looked at everything that had 'failed' at previous conferences, especially in Seattle, and analysed what they would need to 'adjust'.

Some 8,829 tasks were identified and brought together in a meta-Mind Map. They then Mind Mapped all the possible areas of conflict and the ways in which they could be contained peacefully.

After this, they Mind Mapped the intentions and plans of the anti-globalization protesters, and contacted their organizations. They shared with them these Mind Maps in order to break down the 'them and us' barriers.

Rather than have the protesters disrupt the residents of Cancun, the Mexican authorities promised them accommodation and interview time with the media to communicate their case. What do you think happened next?

# SUCCESS, SUCCESS, SUCCESS!

→ The event took place without a single act of violence of one person against another

→ The leaders of the anti-globalization movement expressed their appreciation at what the organizers of the conference did for them

→ There was a high level of cooperation between two traditionally opposing factions

→ A 200-page document based on how Mind Maps played a key role in the planning and implementation of the event was drawn up.

→ This document is now used as an operations manual and blueprint for how to manage other major international events facing a similar threat of violence

Mind Maps in combination with the principles of the TEFCAS model are a powerful mechanism for success.

This last element of **TEFCAS** is so important that it rises in prominence to the level of a third Brain Principle.

The success principle is the culmination of TEFCAS and is your brain's survival-based fundamental mechanism for building successful Mind Map patterns of thought as you progress and succeed through life.

# The Principle of Success

Brain principle 3 – your brain is a success mechanism

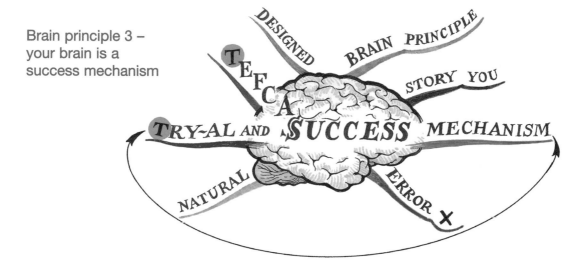

As discussed in Chapter Two, your brain operates *synergetically* and learns and grows through *repetition*. A third important principle for you to understand is that your brain is a *success* **mechanism**.

In the last few decades of the 20th-century psychologists and thinkers described the brain as a trial and error mechanism. This phrase was meant to explain that the brain learned primarily by experimentation, but it contained within it a dangerous Meta-Negative Thought – the brain was error-directed. If the brain were, as the phrase implies, a trial and error mechanism, you would have been born, and tried: error, error, error, error, and within a few minutes it would have all been over!

The truth of the matter is that you were born and you tried: success, success, success, success, ERROR! ('Emergency! Check the Feedback and immediately Adjust! Redirect the goals toward the Success of survival!') Try again! Success, success, success, success, ERROR! ('Check Feedback, Adjust to Success, try again.') Success, success, success, success, and so on for the rest of your life.

*The person who never made a mistake, never tried anything new.*

**Albert Einstein**

Your life has been a constant tale of success against the most incredible odds. You are, in every sense of the words, a success story!

To check the emotional and meta-thinking accuracy of these findings, repeat to yourself for about a minute: 'I am a trial and error mechanism,' 'I am a trial and error mechanism,' 'I am a trial and error mechanism.' How does it feel? And what effect does it begin to have on your emotions, body, and poise?

Now repeat the affirmation 'I am a success mechanism,' 'I am a success mechanism,' 'I am a success mechanism.' Again, how do your body and mind physically begin to respond?

Your brain is a success mechanism. When you are successful your body and all your senses open.

**You are designed for success!**

# The Prime Learning Goal – the Correct Formula

In view of all of the above, let's look again at the world's most popular goal: 'To get better with every trial'. Can you now find the fault in this affirmation?

It has one fatal flaw: the word 'every'. As you now know, it is impossible in the physical universe to learn anything without experimenting. When you experiment you take risks. And when you take risks, at some stage you are inevitably going to make mistakes! By setting the goal of getting better with every trial, individuals have doomed themselves to inevitable failure.

There must be another way ...

If we can't 'get better' with every trial, what must the new goal be?

**'To learn with every trial!'**

This goal is completely compatible with the way your Mind Map patterns of thought and the Universe naturally work.

 *A man's errors are his portals of discovery.*

**James Joyce**

# Analysing a Global Thinking Error

Armed with our knowledge of **TEFCAS** and our new goal to learn with every trial, let us revisit our poor learning friend, whom we left stranded in the slough of despond at the 96th Big Black Hole trial.

Looked at in our new **TEFCAS** and learning context, is this trial a failure? No, it is not! What is it? It is simply another event. Do such events inevilably happen? Yes they do. Are they part of the learning process? Yes they are. Do they fit in with the concept of **TEFCAS**, learning and experimentation? Yes they do.

These events are part of the natural learning processes of your brain, and they are inevitably going to occur. Should we fear them? Obviously not. When they do occur should we swear, rant, rave, and get ourselves into a Meta-Negative Thinking spiral? Again, obviously not.

We suddenly enter a Paradigm Shift in thinking about learning where we realize that the entire global reaction to failure, and all the fear, stress, and disease associated with it, are all the product of thought, thought based on a slightly incorrect formula about how the brain should set its goals, and how it should therefore be taught to learn.

So, with our new understanding of **TEFCAS** and the learning formula, how should we react to that 96th Trial? Rather than falling into despondency, we adjust our verbal response from expletives to the more helpful and positive 'How fascinating!' This leaves our senses far more open to the experience, and allows us to get the full and valuable Feedback from what was once called a 'failure', and which we now realize is simply another Event.

Many people report that, some time after a major Big Black Hole, they realize that it was this Event that gave them major new insights and strengths. Has it been the same with you?

After having Checked the Feedback from our Big Black Hole, what are we obliged to do next? Adjust toward our positive goal of Success and try again. As you continue applying your **TEFCAS** Success Formula, you will inevitably rise and fall as you progress. If, however, you persist, you will, also inevitably, suddenly experience the opposite of the Big Black Hole: the giant Star of Success!

However, even Success holds its own dangers. Some love this triumph so much that they are afraid to try again, for fear that they will never return to such giddy heights. Some set their goals too low and too much in the short term, and suddenly, to their despair, find that they have nowhere left to go.

**In a recent Olympic semi-final, one of the runners in the 400 metres had made it to the final. He was interviewed after the race, and exclaimed ecstatically: 'This is amazing! It's fantastic! I've always wanted to be in the Olympic final! It's my dream come true!' And off he happily jogged.**

**What do you think happened to him in the final? Last! Why? Because his brain and body had already done what he had instructed them to do – get him to the Olympic final. The goal was already reached. Once he was in the final it didn't matter what he did – he could have walked – because he was there. In the final, you could see that all his motivation had gone.**

What does the **TEFCAS** Brain Success Formula say you should do after a major Success? Celebrate, obviously, and then, as you did with every other Trial, say 'How fascinating!' Check that Success, gather all the valuable information from those amazing internal Mind Map thought patterns of yours, Adjust toward your far-reaching goals, and Try again.

When you continue to apply the Success Formula and persist in your Trying, you will inevitably create more and more Successes.

## Mind Map Exercise: a Success Story

Using the six steps of the TEFCAS model as your main branches, draw a Mind Map of a success, or a series of successes, with which you are particularly pleased. Think about the process you went through – this could be the way in which you planned or adjustments that you made to your plan as you put it into action – before you arrived at your successful outcome.

For example, on your 'FEEDBACK' branch, did you assess how things were progressing as you went along? Did you realize that you needed to make a few adjustments to your action plan before you could achieve your goal? What was it? Really investigate what you could see was working and what you thought needed improvement.

Mind Mapping a success story in this way will help you see how your established achievements already correspond to the TEFCAS Success Formula for learning. It will also help you to identify the elements of your success that led to your achieving your goal. This means that you can use them to help you succeed next time and the next and the next. But what about if you haven't had the outcome you wanted? What if you have 'FAILED'? **In order to turn 'failure' into success you need to combine the principles of the TEFCAS model with PERSISTENCE.**

# The Principle of Persistence

The whole **TEFCAS** model assumes throughout the presence of a mental quality that is so important that it, like the Success Principle, has risen to the status of another Brain Principle: PERSISTENCE. The principle of persistence is designed to help you establish permanent, stronger, and bigger internal Mind Map patterns of thought.

> *If you never give up, you are a winner.*
>
> John Akhwari, last in the 1968 Mexico City Olympic marathon, after battling through serious injury and exhaustion to finish the race

Persistence has often been seen not as a characteristic of intelligence, but as a characteristic of the opposite of intelligence. Those who display persistence are often labelled 'stubborn', 'inflexible', and any one of the various 'headeds': 'pig ...', 'bull ...', 'thick ...', 'hard ...'!

Not only is this not the case, the very opposite is true.

Persistence is, in fact, the engine of learning and intelligence when it comes to your Mind Maps of thought. It is the engine of all creative effort, and of all genius. Most importantly, it is the Try in **TEFCAS**.

**T**ry, try, try and try again!
**E**
**F**
**C**
**A**
**S**

The importance of Persistence was summed up best by the most productive creative mind of the last 300 years, Thomas Edison, who holds the record for the largest number of individual patents registered (see also pp. 126–7). As well as being famous for his invention of the light bulb (among many other things), Edison is equally renowned for his famous quotation about genius:

*Genius is one percent inspiration; ninety-nine percent perspiration.*

**Perspiration = Persistence!**

# PERSISTENCE AND 'THE GREATEST OLYMPIAN OF THEM ALL'

In the sport of rowing, there is a motto which most of the great rowers live by: 'Miles Makes Champions'. It is the Persistence of regular practice, both on and off the water, which is the 'secret formula' that leads to the Olympic Gold.

Perhaps one of the greatest ever examples of Persistence, into a training discipline and ritual that produced one of the greatest body and mind performances in history, is that of Sir Steve Redgrave, CBE. Redgrave achieved the almost unbelievable feat of winning gold medals in *five* consecutive Olympic Games, in one of the toughest of all sports – rowing. His outstanding achievements represented 20 years of extraordinary commitment to a vision of excellence and to a training ritual of unparalleled intensity.

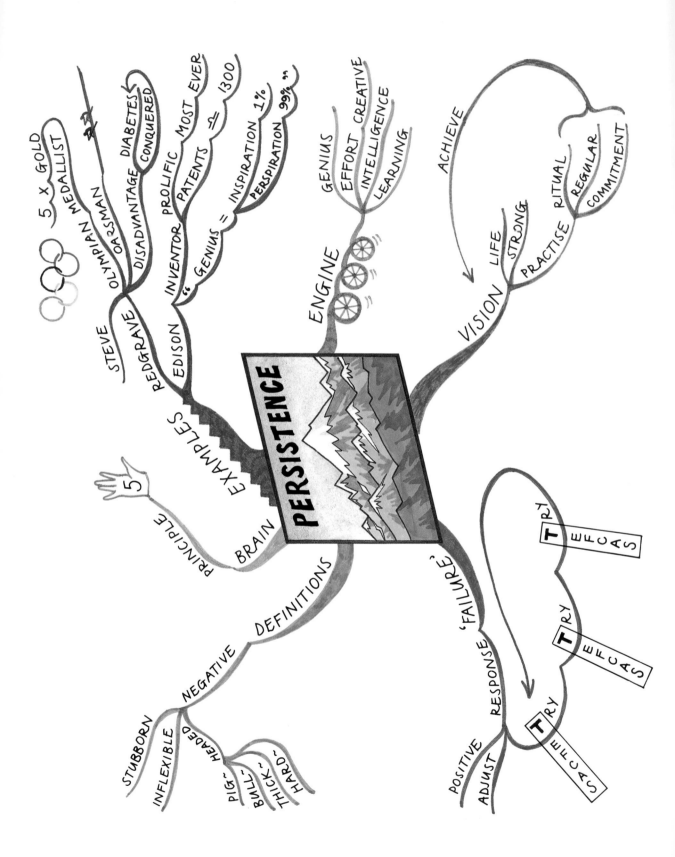

# Mind Map Exercise: from Failure to Success

This time draw a Mind Map, again based on the TEFCAS model for your main branches about a time when you failed.

On your 'TRIAL' branch, add sub-branches about what it was you were trying to achieve – your goal – and what it was that you actually tried.

Next, think about what the 'EVENT' was. What happened? What went wrong? What went to plan?

Now develop your 'FEEDBACK' branch. If at this point you gave up it could be that you didn't assess what went wrong. Now you need to. Did you plan the event thoroughly? Were you properly informed? Did you ask other people involved for ideas about why things didn't go to plan? What did they say? Feedback is a vital stage of learning and you need to be as objective about it as possible to ensure success in the future.

Next look at your 'CHECK' branch. What lessons did you learn from the feedback you got? Did you need to brush up on some skills? Did you need to plan better? Should you have had a back-up plan to respond more flexibly to the outcome?

On your fifth branch, 'ADJUST', explore what you need to do next time to turn your failure into a success. Would you need to train more to be fitter on the day? Will you spend more time learning your material or planning the event? What are you going to do next time to avoid the pitfalls from the first time you tried? Are you starting to see how you will be able to SUCCEED next time?

Finally, explore the 'SUCCESS' branch of your Mind Map. What will you have achieved when you succeed next time? How will you feel about yourself when you do? What will you have learned?

# Mind Maps and TEFCAS

Mind Maps are an excellent way to explore your successes and your successes-in-progress within the TEFACS model. They will help you objectively to assess what is working and what is not, to learn from your 'events,' and to plan for your next success.

The Mind Map opposite sums up the **TEFCAS** model and clearly breaks down each stage of the model for you. Keep referring back to it to help you assess where you are on your road to success, and draw your own Mind Maps of the situation in hand to brainstorm your strategy.

In Chapter Two we looked at the key learning principles of synergy and repetition and in this chapter we have investigated the principles of success and persistence through the **TEFCAS** model. We have also seen that Mind Maps are an extremely brain-friendly tool that encourage synergetic thinking and make it easy for us to plan for and analyse our successes.

The next chapter puts into action this new awareness of our brain and its amazing innate capacity for success. It will show you how to use Mind Maps to unlock the power of your brain and fulfil your true potential.

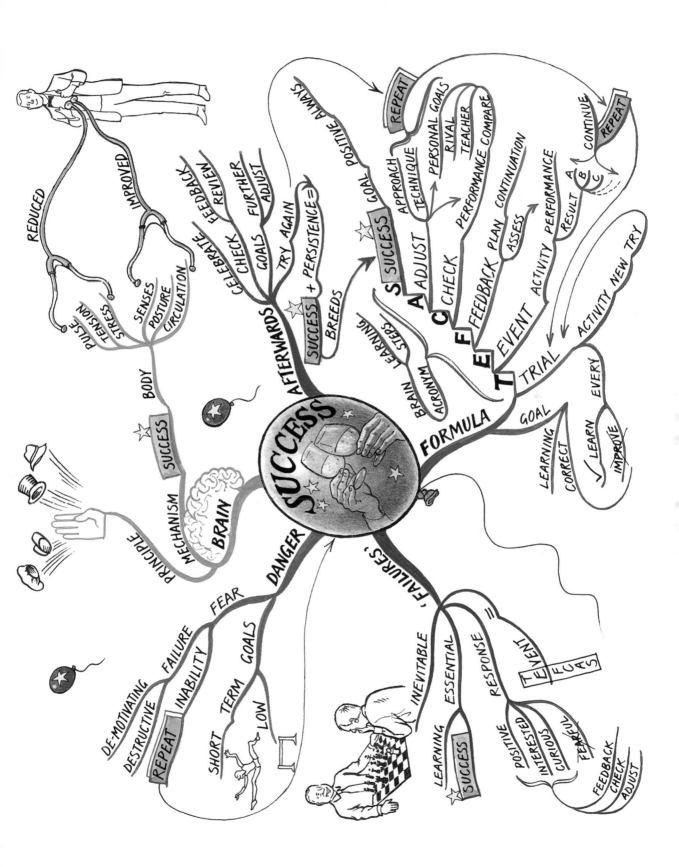

# Mind Workouts for Mental Success

*Ideas do not fall from the sky; they come from people. People write the software. People design the products. People start the new businesses. Every new thinking that gives us pleasure or productivity or convenience, be it an iPod or the tweaks that make a chemical plant more efficient, is the result of human ingenuity.*

*Harvard Business Review, October 2004*

# Overview of Chapter 4:

Great advances in the world have always developed out of ideas and the world relies on brains like yours to make great leaps forward. What does it take to come up with the best ideas? Creativity. A Mind Map is the ultimate creative-thinking tool – it acts as a gymnasium for your creativity. In this chapter we will explore the essences of creative thinking on which Mind Maps are based.

You are inherently creative and if you don't believe this it is probably because the way you were educated or conditioned has made it difficult for you to tap into this ability. How creative you are plays a vital role in your capacity to come up with new ideas, to solve problems in original ways, and to stand head and shoulders above the crowd in terms of imagination, behaviour, and productivity. If you can fully unlock your innate creativity you will understand that your potential to achieve and succeed is limitless.

So what exactly is creativity? Creativity is your ability to think in new ways – to be original. Creative thinking includes:

**Fluency** – the speed and ease with which you can 'rattle off' new and creative ideas.

**Flexibility** – your ability to see things from different angles, to consider things from the opposite point of view, to take old concepts and rearrange them in new ways, and to reverse pre-existing ideas. It also includes your ability to use all your senses in the creation of new ideas.

**Originality** – this is at the heart of all creative thinking, and represents your ability to produce ideas that are unique, unusual, and 'eccentric', literally 'away from the centre'. Although many people think such a person is 'uncontrolled', exactly the opposite is true: originality often results from a great deal of directed intellectual energy, and it generally shows a capacity for high levels of concentration.

To be original you need to get away from the norm. Normal means average – it is a level of thinking to which your brain has become accustomed; that which gives you no surprises; that which remains the same; that which no longer shocks, startles, surprises or provokes you; that which does not stretch your imagination.

To create means virtually the opposite: to bring into existence something new, fresh, and original – to give rise to, to establish an association that has never been established before.

*Thomas Edison, the man famed for inventing the light bulb, was a creative genius when it came to ideas. He patented over 1,000 different inventions in his lifetime!*

**Thomas Edison – creative genius extraordinaire**

Expanding on ideas – the creative thinker is able to build on, develop, embroider, embellish, and generally elaborate and expand upon ideas.

# How Can I Boost My Creativity?

To liberate your creative potential you need to foster a thinking environment for your brain that liberates its synergetic way of thinking. As you will recall from Chapter Two, your brain does not think linearly or sequentially like a computer, but radiantly and explosively as shown in the diagram below.

Your brain thinks radiantly and explosively

Creative thinking involves the use of the full range of left- and right-brain mental skills, including:

| Left Brain | Right Brain |
|---|---|
| Words | Rhythm |
| Logic | Spatial awareness |
| Numbers | Gestalt (whole picture) |
| Sequence | Imagination |
| Linearity | Daydreaming |
| Analysis | Colour |
| Lists | Dimension |

Education systems tend to focus on left-brain skills and place less emphasis on right-brain skills, which immediately impacts on our capacity to think creatively. If your academic background has developed your verbal, mathematical, and analytical abilities but neglected skills such as drawing, painting, and music – or vice versa – the chances are you are only tapping in to a fraction of your creative capabilities. What do you get when you combine the left and right skills of the brain? A Mind Map! A Mind Map includes each aspect of the left and right cortexes and is therefore a superb whole-brained thinking tool.

# Creativity is a 'by definition' awareness:

- If **Alexander the Great** had fought his battles in the way that all the people before had fought them, he would neither have survived nor would we have ever heard of him.

- If **Beethoven** had composed music in exactly the same style as Haydn, he would now be noted as a minor composer, not a giant among giants.

- If **Elizabeth I** of England had accepted the normal restrictions society placed upon women at that time, she would never have become one of the greatest rulers England has ever seen.

- If **Picasso** had painted only like van Gogh, he would have been considered simply as a copyist and irrelevant to the history of art, rather than a towering presence in the pantheon of artistic genius.

- If the greatest athlete of the 20th century, **Muhammed Ali**, had boxed like the average boxer, he would, literally, have been knocked out of our consciousness!

Mind Maps are the one tool you can rely on to help you think expansively, to think creatively. Whenever you need to come up with an idea, to plan something with ingenuity, or to unlock your imagination, get out a blank piece of paper and Mind Map your thoughts.

## Charles Darwin

**Darwin was a Mind Mapper!** In developing his Theory of Evolution, Charles Darwin had a vast task in front of him: he had to explore as much of the natural world as possible; to classify each of the species and their relationships to each other; to explain the regularities and 'irregularities' in nature; to demonstrate the explosive and multiplicative nature of growth and diversity. How did he do this? With basic Mind Maps!

Darwin devised a basic Mind Map form of notes, which was very much like a branching tree. Darwin used these basic Mind Map forms as the only effective way to help him collect masses of data, to organize it, to see the relationships between the various items, and to create new awarenesses from it.

**It is reported that within 15 months of drawing his first tree 'Mind Map' diagram, Darwin had worked out all the major components of the Theory of Evolution.**

Illustration of Darwin's note-taking method

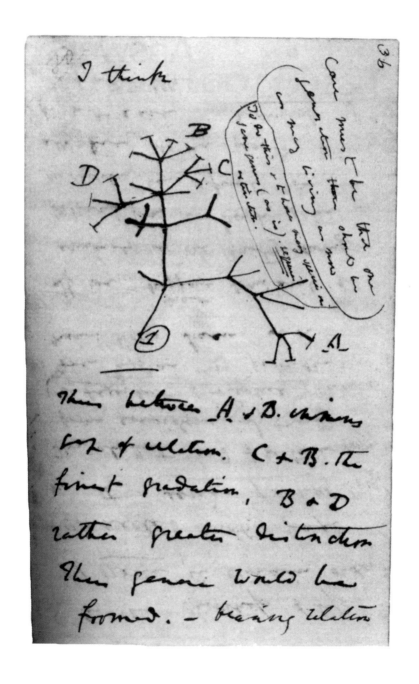

## Creativity Test

Give yourself exactly two minutes to write down, as fast as you can, *in list form*, every single use you can think of for a coat-hanger. Then divide the number by two to calculate your number-of-uses-per-minute score.

# Global Average Results

The average-number-of-uses-for-a-coat-hanger-per-minute scores range from 0 (and this is with some effort!) through 4–5 (which is the global average), to 8 (which is good 'brain-stormer' level), 12 (which is exceptional and rare), to 16 – which is Thomas Edison-genius level.

If people are given as long as they want to think up as many uses as they can for a coat-hanger, the average score is 20–30 uses.

Recalling all that you have learned so far about your wonderful, amazing brain, doesn't something here strike you as a little odd?

Imagine that you are a salesperson, who is trying to convince a customer to 'buy brains'.

You go through all your sales patter – you tell them that you have the most amazing product in the universe. You explain that each brain is a super-bio-computer and each has a million million super-bio-computer microchips. You point out that the number of patterns of intelligence your company's brains can make is the number one followed by ten-and-a-half million kilometres of zeros.

You go on to mention that these particular brains can remember virtually anything as long as they use special memory techniques, showing off their ability to link any object with any other object. You throw in that your superb product can think, speak multiple languages, solve mathematical problems, see, hear, smell, taste, touch, and operate its associated body magnificently.

Finally you reach the climax of your presentation, and inform the customer that this amazing product can think of four or five uses for a coat-hanger in a minute, and about 25 in a lifetime! Sale closed?!

# FURTHER EXAMINATION OF THE CREATIVITY TEST

Go back to your original uses for your coat-hanger and circle the one you think is your most creative idea. When you have chosen it, jot down the criteria that made you choose it. You chose it because it was the most ... what?

Now check the following list of words and mark the ones you think best define an idea that is creative:

a)   Normal

b)   Original

c)   Practical

d)   Removed from the norm

e)   Bland

f)   Exciting

The obvious answers are that creative ideas need to be original and removed from the norm, and, as such, they are usually exciting.

If you come up with the idea that you could use a coat-hanger to hang coats on, no one is going to beat a path to your door! However, if you thought of using it to form sculptures, or to make a musical instrument, people will be far more interested not only in your ideas, but in you too.

If you think about it, the great geniuses, by definition, had to be 'removed from the norm'. If Stravinsky had written music like all those before him, we would never have heard of him. Similarly if Picasso had painted like his predecessors, instead of in his astoundingly original style, we also would never have known of him.

## LOOKING AGAIN AT THE CREATIVITY TEST

Let's look again at the question – 'Think of every possible use you can for a coat-hanger.'

The more rigidly taught mind will assume that 'uses' refer to the standard, ordinary, sensible applications for a coat-hanger. That same rigidly taught mind will also assume that the coat-hanger is of a standard size and is made of the standard material. Standard, standard, standard = normal, normal, normal thinking. And norm-al thinking is average. Remember, the very word 'normal' was born from the statistical 'norm'.

What is the Creativity Test trying to measure? Thoughts that are original, away from the norm.

The mentally literate, and therefore more flexibly taught, brain will see far more opportunities for creative interpretations of the question, and therefore will generate both more ideas, and ideas of higher quality. The mentally literate and creative mind will expand the meaning of the word 'uses' to include the phrase 'connections with'. It will also realize immediately that the coat-hanger could be of any size, made of any material, and be transformed into any shape.

The creative genius will therefore break all the ordinary boundaries, and will include in the list of uses, many 'far out' applications, such as 'melting a five-ton metal coat-hanger and pouring it into a giant mold to make the hull of a boat'.

As you can see, the mentally literate, creative individual is naturally tapping in to the brain's basic physical capacity to make one-followed-by-ten-and-a-half-million-kilometres-of-zeros-worth of associations.

A mere 2,000 or so uses for any standard object, to such a mind, is only the start!

## The Creative Mind Map – the Ultimate Creative-Thinking Tool

From what you know about the brain's synergetic thinking, about its infinitely associative physical pathways, and about its creative capacity to form links and associations in all directions, you will realize that linear note-taking and list-making is the worst way you can choose to encourage your brain's creativity! Lines and lists put your brain behind prison bars that methodically disconnect and cut off each thought from every other thought. It is like taking a pair of scissors and snipping the connections between your brain cells.

**Mind Maps are a creative-thinking tool that reflect your brain's natural way of functioning. They allow it to use all its images and associations in the explosive and networking way to which it was born, which internally it always uses, and to which you need to allow it to become re-accustomed.**

# Mind Map creativity game

To test for yourself that this concept is true – that your own and anyone else's creative thinking can be taught and improved – try the following new Creativity Test, this time using a Mind Map. Brainstorming with a Mind Map will help you explore associations and images – both of which are fundamental building blocks of Mind Maps. Remember, think out of the box, think originally.

Listed below are 30 randomly generated words. Your task is to find uses and/or associations between a coat-hanger and each of the listed words. You could of course play this game with your friends, as more minds means more ideas.

Some of these may seem difficult at first, but if you persevere and look for wider and wilder interpretations, you will find an association. Really let your imagination run riot on your Mind Maps!

At the end of the list you will find examples thought up by my students, friends and myself. If you come up with ideas that are more 'far out' than ours, give yourself some extra congratulations!

**Enjoy the journey into your newly creative imagination!**

1.  Golf ball
2.  Snow
3.  Lock
4.  Muscle
5.  Mussel
6.  Music
7.  Circus
8.  Back
9.  Plant
10. Flag
11. Shoe
12. Potato
13. Pipe
14. Pen
15. Solar system
16. Knife
17. Money
18. Clock
19. Ice
20. Animal
21. Soup bowl
22. Light bulb
23. Salt
24. Hair
25. Communication
26. Drinking straw
27. Tree
28. Fish
29. Juggling
30. Ship

# POSSIBLE ASSOCIATIONS AND/OR USES FOR THE LIST OF 30

1. **Golf ball.** The coat-hanger could be used to retrieve golf balls from unfriendly ponds or ditches. A large coat-hanger could be moulded into an extra golf club in cases of emergency.

2. **Snow.** By lashing leather around it, you could transform a coat-hanger into a snow shoe. By lashing some more solid object into its triangular 'window' you could fashion a primitive ski or sled.

3. **Lock.** A coat-hanger could make a perfect key or lock-opener (indeed, creative crooks often use them as tools for breaking into vehicles!).

4. **Muscle.** A coat-hanger of a thick resilient material such as silicon or reinforced rubber could be used as an isometric muscle-training device.

5. **Mussel.** A coat-hanger could make a perfect tool for both opening the shell of the mussel and for scooping out the meat within.

6. **Music.** The coat-hanger is a ready-made triangle!

7. **Circus.** A coat-hanger could be used as the hoop through which animals jump. The size of the coat-hanger would depend upon the size of the animal ...

8. **Back.** Scratcher!

9. **Plant.** A coat-hanger would make an idea plant trainer.

10. **Flag.** A coat-hanger could act as a flagpole. It could also be used to keep the furled flag in place.

11. **Shoe.** An ideal shoe horn!

12. **Potato.** A perfect spit for holding your baking potato over the blazing flames.

13. **Pipe.** Cleaner!

14. **Pen.** Use your coat-hanger to scratch messages on rock; to write messages in clay; or you could file the end off at an angle, dip it in ink, and use it as a standard pen.

15. **Solar system.** Use your coat-hanger to hang models of the sun and the nine planets from a schoolroom ceiling, in order to teach the children about the local neighborhood of our universe.

16. **Knife.** A coat-hanger can easily be transformed into a cutting device.

17. **Money.** Use a coat-hanger to barter with if someone desperately needs one, or use a gold coat-hanger to trade for anything you want!

18. **Clock.** By sticking a coat-hanger upright in the ground, you can use it as a sun dial, the casting of its shadow accurately telling you the time.

19. **Ice.** A super-cooled coat-hanger could be used to make ice.

20. **Animal.** A coat-hanger could be an animal's toy, or could be used to release a trapped animal.

21. **Soup bowl.** A big coat-hanger made of metal could be pounded flat and then easily sculpted into a soup bowl.

22. **Light bulb.** A coat-hanger could be used as the filament in a bulb.

23. **Salt**. A coat-hanger is an ideal instrument for unclogging the salt shaker or for separating the particles in salt that has become clumped.

24. **Hair**. The point of the coat-hanger could be used as a primitive and simple comb. The whole coat-hanger could also be used as a foundation piece for a punk-rocker's hair-do!

25. **Communication**. An ideal instrument for tapping out the Morse code.

26. **Drinking straw**. A thick coat-hanger could be tunneled out, and would immediately be useful as a straw.

27. **Tree**. Coat-hangers are made for clothes trees!

28. **Fish**. Hook.

29. **Juggling**. If jugglers can juggle with balls, flaming clubs, guns, chickens and chain-saws, why not coat-hangers?!

30. **Ship**. Anchor. Rudder. Sail clip. All-purpose tool. (You should never sail without one!)

# Creative Observations

A number of lessons can be learned from this exercise:

1.  That the way to stimulate your creative imagination is not to spend time looking for a possible use or association. This is just a case of searching in an infinite darkness. The correct way is to give your brain any other item. With the two in place your brain will automatically go into 'Synergetic Association Mode', and will, inevitably, find a link.

2.  That if you apply this second, correct formula, your brain can link anything with anything – this exercise has just demonstrated your brain's infinite capacity to create associations and to generate creative thought.

    Leonardo da Vinci, the man most often regarded the greatest creative genius of all time, said that one of the principles by which he operated, and by which he generated his own creative thinking, was the observation that: ***'Everything in some way connects to everything else.'***

3.  We also learn from this exercise that when you do give your brain items to link, it will associate them together with accelerating speed. Your brain can be trained to improve!

4.  In addition you will have observed that the more you use this 'paired association' technique for creative thinking, the more wild and far out your ideas will become. And in the context of creativity, what do 'wild and far out' mean? Good quality creativity!

A further realization from this last point is that creative thinking leads to humour and the probability of more humour! Humour is one of the hallmarks of the creative mind – develop your wit and you will be improving the power of your creative intelligence.

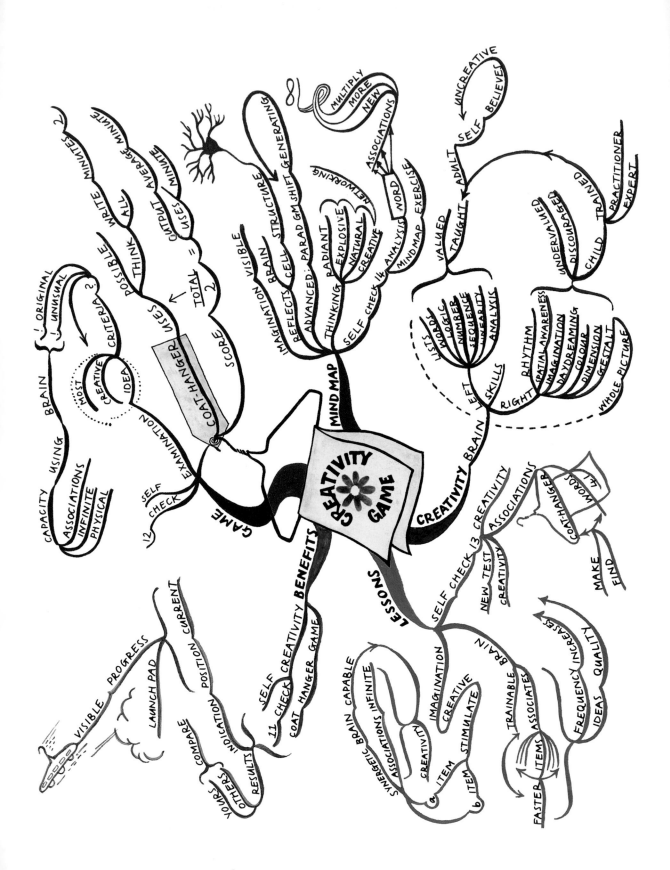

# Mind Maps for Creative Thinking

The coat-hanger exercise is, of course, just a game but it is a game with a serious purpose: it plays with your imagination. To be creative you have to unlock your imagination and, as you have seen, Mind Maps help you do just that. Mind Maps are an excellent tool for strengthening your ability to make associations and create images in the Mind Maps of your thoughts.

Mind Maps encourage creativity – if you want to come up with brilliant ideas, find inspired solutions to any problem or find new ways to motivate yourself and others, you need to set your imagination free with Mind Maps.

**Mind Maps will help you:**

➡ increase your speed of thinking

➡ give you infinite flexibility

➡ explore the outer reaches of your thinking where original ideas abide

# Mind Map Example: Problem-Solving

Imagine that you are the manager of a successful chain of music stores called *The Beat Master*. You have just found out that *High Friction*, an aggressive competitor from the other side of town, intends to open up a number of new stores, each within two minutes of your own. You have three months to prepare your strategy to protect your revenues and to ensure that you retain your customers. Draw a Mind Map to brainstorm your plan of action.

Start by drawing an image in the centre of your Mind Map that represents *The Beat Master* triumphing over *High Friction*. This might be your company logo dominating that of your competitor. It is important to start out with the attitude that you will face off this new competition – if you don't, you will put yourself on the path to failure!

Take a minute to think about the main issues you need to investigate and add your main branches to your Mind Map. These might be 'customers', 'Beat Master', 'High Friction', and 'Strategy'.

Next explore your main branches with sub-branches and sub-sub-branches. For example, on your 'customers' branch, define who your customers are. Why do you think people choose to buy their music with you? How do you keep them satisfied? What do you offer your customers that other stores do not? Do you encourage your customers to give you regular feedback? If so, what is it and have you responded to it? Do you know the kind of customers that visit the High Friction stores on the other side of town? If you don't, add a sub-branch to your 'strategy' branch to make sure you find out.

When you develop the main branch about your chain of stores, really explore what you think works well and what you think you could improve. This should be at every level, from the experience of your staff and the service they offer your customers to the look and feel of your stores. Are you sure that the layout of your stores is as customer-friendly as possible? If you think that your stores are a bit shabby or poorly organized, add a plan for renovations to your strategy branch. How competitively priced is your music? Could you or should you offer a wider range of music? If so, add that to your strategy branch.

Keep exploring each of your main branches until you have explored every angle of the situation. You can also use the strategy branch to plan a time-frame for all your action points. You may find that your Mind Map outgrows your piece of paper; if so, tape more sheets together and keep going! **If you get into the habit of brainstorming problems in this way you will find it easier and easier to unlock your imagination and come up with creative solutions for the situation in hand.**

As you implement your strategies, make sure that you use the **TEFCAS** success formula (see Chapter Three) to monitor your progress and adapt to any changes in the situation.

For more examples of how you can use Mind Maps for greater mental success, turn to Chapter Six.

# Advanced Creative Mind Mapping – Generating the Paradigm Shift

As you explore any subject with a creative Mind Map you will see that words which initially did not seem particularly significant will occasionally pop up on the outer limits of one branch, and then another, and then another.

If such a word or concept appears twice, simply underline it in each instance, to make it stand out from the background. Should that same word pop up a third time, it is probably worth putting a small box around it, as it is obviously of growing importance, and certainly deserves more emphasis than words that appear only once.

In certain instances you will find a word that appears on four or more branches, or even on all the branches of your developing creative Mind Map. If this happens, put the box into three dimensions.

At this stage you can use your cortical skills of dimension and Gestalt (your brain's ability to see the 'whole picture') to help bring about a major shift and advance in your thinking on the subject. First you dimensionalize the boxes around the key concept. Next you link the boxes to form a giant box; and then you dimensionalize that box.

In what does your original Mind Map now nestle? A new framework. In other words, your mind has realized that the original network of thought is actually contained within a larger framework, and that a word or concept you originally thought was minor is, in fact, so major that it pervades your subject, and may well warrant being made the new centre for your next creative Mind Map on the topic.

This is called a ***Paradigm Shift*** in thinking, and it is the goal of all great thinkers. Beethoven paradigm-shifted our appreciation of emotion and music; Cézanne paradigm-shifted the perception of all artists after him; Magellan paradigm-shifted the flat earth to a global planet; Copernicus paradigm-shifted the universe inside out; Einstein paradigm-shifted our perceptions of the nature of that universe.

The creative-thinking Mind Map is a thinking tool designed to accelerate the appearance of Paradigm Shifts, and thus to enhance the global output of creative thought. Use it to enhance your own creativity, and as a constant reminder of just how infinite your creative-thinking capabilities are.

# Creativity and Memory

To become a creative genius you need to let your imagination run wild and to encourage your brain to make new and stronger associations between the ideas it already has and the ideas it is freshly generating. However, when you develop your creative skills you are not just improving your ability to come up with innovative ideas and inspired solutions: strong creative skills by default enhance your ability to remember things. This is because creativity and memory are virtually identical mental processes – they both work best when you use imagination and association.

 **If you really want to make leaps forward and boost your memory powers, you need to actively use imagination and association when you want to remember something.**

# A Creative Star

Richard Branson definitely did not breeze through school, as you might have expected – he was severely dyslexic and struggled with books throughout his academic career, being so embarrassed by his lack of ability in reading that he spent hours memorizing texts word-for-word whenever he knew he would have to read in public. His IQ scores were low and to his teachers he was obviously not bright.

How did Richard Branson get from the unpromising position he was in as a child, to become the mastermind behind over 150 enterprises that carry the Virgin® name, with a personal wealth estimated to be approximately three billion pounds?

What the IQ test had failed to measure was his burning ambition, which drove him on to find creative solutions no matter what the problems were, and to keep persisting where others would have given up long before. Those tests also never identified his ability to share his creative visions and dreams with others, and to blend their dreams with his.

As a teenager, Richard Branson became increasingly frustrated (as all creative people do!) with the rigidity of school rules and regulations. His first act of creative rebellion was to start his own student newspaper.

*A dyslexic starting a newspaper?!*

*Yes!*

The original way in which Branson directed his newspaper was that instead of focussing it on the school, he decided to take the opposite view and focus on the students. Rather than being a standard fuddy-duddy and boring 'rag', Richard wanted his newspaper to be colourful and exciting, appealing to everyone, and especially to major corporations who would buy advertising!

Branson decided to break the mold by having not just student journalists, but by inviting rock stars, movie celebrities, MPs, creative 'names', and sports stars to contribute.

Richard and his co-editor friend Johnnie Gems did not, however, start penniless. They had £4 to help cover postage and telephone expenses, donated by his mum! The two boys worked in the Bransons' basement and scrimped and saved wherever possible – though not on their grand creative dream, which remained their driving force.

Prophetically, Richard Branson's headmaster (who was also obviously beginning to recognize that the IQ tests may have been wrong), said to him one day: 'Congratulations, Branson. I predict that you will either go to prison or become a millionaire.'

From that time on, Branson expanded on his original idea, spinning off new companies, creating new products, devising new ideas, and continually appealing to the dreams of others. His flagship company, Virgin Airlines, is a perfect example of creativity in action. Instead of getting caught in the downward spiral of chopping fares and cutting service, he again decided to reverse normal thinking, by maintaining fares but *improving* service, which included such strikingly original ideas as in-flight massages, ice-cream with movies, showers, exercise facilities, and private bedrooms.

Richard Branson himself, known as a flamboyant, colourful, and extraordinarily creative human being, attributes his success to his ability to generate and follow great creative visions, and his ability to recognize the same in others and to have them all, as a team, follow their dreams.

# Creative Productivity

Fluency in creative thinking refers to the number of ideas that you can create, and the speed at which you create them. Fluency is one of the main goals of all creative thinkers and of all the great geniuses.

This goal can itself create a problem – that of quality. What happens to the quality of your creative ideas if you start to speed up your thinking and generate greater numbers of ideas? Does the quality go down, stay the same, or go up?

The answer, surprisingly (and mercifully!) is that as the quantity and speed of the ideas goes up, the overall quality of ideas goes up too.

In other words, in creative thinking, you can have your cake and eat it too!

Look at the great creative thinkers opposite, and see how this process worked for them. The sheer volume and productivity of some of these great thinkers is astounding.

→ **Marie Curie**, the great scientist, was awarded not just one Nobel Prize, but two – and in two different subjects, physics and chemistry. Her work ranged over the fields of magnetism, radioactivity, and the development of the medical uses of x-rays, and she isolated the chemical elements radium and polonium.

→ **Leonardo da Vinci** created so many ideas in so many different fields that no one has yet counted them all!

➔ **Charles Darwin**, the creator of the Theory of Evolution, not only wrote a 1,000+ page book on this subject; he wrote **119** other scientific papers, books, and booklets.

➔ **Thomas Edison** registered **1,093** original patents, which is still the world record for the greatest number of patents registered by one person. He also completed **350** notebooks of work and ideas.

➔ **Albert Einstein**, in addition to his masterful treatise on Relativity, published over **248** other scientific papers.

➔ **Sigmund Freud** wrote and published over **330** papers on psychology.

➔ **Goethe**, the great German polymath and genius, wrote so prolifically that he used, in all his writings, **50,000** *different* words.

➔ **Garry Kasparov**, the greatest chess player in history, played through, analysed, memorized, and creatively commented on many **thousands** of the world's great chess games.

➔ **Mozart** in his brief lifetime wrote more than **600** pieces of musical genius, including **40** complete symphonies.

➔ **Pablo Picasso**, the creative giant of the 20th century, produced more than **20,000** artistic works.

➔ **Rembrandt**, who was involved in many activities including business, completed in addition to these activities more than **650** paintings and **2,000** drawings.

➔ **William Shakespeare**, the creative genius generally considered to be the greatest English writer of all time, wrote, in a period of about 20 years, **154** sonnets and **37** masterpiece plays.

# Quantity Creates Quality

The list on the previous page blows out of the water the common misconception that geniuses produce only a few precious ideas and then run out of (creative) steam. The opposite is obviously true: they generate vast numbers of ideas, and accelerate their productivity as their lives progress and their creative energy gathers more and more power from all that they have done before.

So did the great creative geniuses simply pour out perfect idea after perfect idea? Absolutely not! What they *did* do was to pour out *ideas*. Many of these were not particularly brilliant, but it was the 'not brilliant' that allowed the brilliant to emerge.

By constantly pouring out ideas, regardless of quality, the great creative geniuses were actually guaranteeing that they *did* produce more quality. They were allowing and facilitating the communication between their left brains and their right brains to produce a synergetic, 'multiplying' thought process that is typical of all those who know how to use their heads!

Our guide to genius, Leonardo, was a perfect example of this. In his notebooks he would literally 'doodle away' with any random thoughts that came to mind, and out of those would leap the 'genius' ideas.

Thomas Edison, Leonardo's great disciple, was identical in his approach. Edison considered creativity to be simply good, honest, and delightful hard work/play. He described creative genius as:

*'1 percent inspiration and 99 percent perspiration.'*

He practised what he preached too: Edison went through **9,000** experiments to perfect the light bulb, and over **50,000** to invent the storage-cell battery.

His attitude towards 'failure' (one we should all copy) was ideal. For example, when he was asked by one of his assistants why he persisted in trying to discover a filament that would last longer in his light bulb, even though he had failed thousands of times, Edison gently pointed out that he hadn't failed once! What he had done was to have discovered thousands of things that didn't work, on his way to finding, inevitably, the one thing that did.

# Gold mining

The creative idea-generating process is very much like panning for gold. Gold flecks are just a few of many thousands of stones or grains of sand that lie in riverbeds. In the river of the mind it is exactly the same. The stones or grains of sand represent all the ideas that are available. To mine for the gold (the great creative idea or new creative solution) you have to sift through *all* the grains (ideas) on the riverbed of your mind to find the real nuggets of value.

The great creative geniuses knew this, and therefore generated hundreds of ideas, sifting out from *them* the real nuggets. Dean Keith Simonton conducted a study of 2,036 creative scientists throughout history, and found what was then surprising, but which to you will now be understandable: the most respected scientists produced not only more great works, but also *more* bad ones than the other scientists.

In other words, the greats simply produced *more* and then selected, from everything, the best.

So now you know the secret of creative productivity: generate more ideas at higher speed, and you will enhance both the quantity and the power of your creative thinking.

# The Power of Imagination

Getting your imagination involved ensures that you are also using the right side of your brain when normally you'd be relying on your left. As you will recall from Chapter Two, if you only engage one side of your brain you drastically reduce the overall performance of your brain.

## Let Your Imagination Help You Remember!

You can engage your imagination in many ways when you are trying to remember something:

→ **Exaggeration.** The more dramatic you can make information you want to remember, the easier it will be to fix it in your memory. This is because you make it more interesting for your lively brain.

→ **Humour.** Like exaggeration, the more ridiculous and outrageous you can make information you are trying to retain, the more it will appeal to your imagination. Humour is the hallmark of a creative mind.

→ **Senses.** You experience your environment with the help of your five senses, sight, touch, smell, hearing, and taste, all of which are strong memory triggers – have you ever smelt a passer-by's perfume and suddenly thought of someone who wears the same scent? Engaging your senses when you want to remember something will help you create a three-dimensional memory of what you want to retain.

→ **Colour.** Try to add colour to whatever you are trying to remember – free your mind from traditional black and white note-taking and use your imagination! Use of vivid colours helps engage your imagination.

→ **Rhythm.** Movement and rhythm are also powerful imagination tools as they will help you create a more real mental picture of what you are trying to learn.

→ **Positive Thinking.** In general, it is easier to remember information that you think of positively and that you like, than information you don't find interesting or think of negatively. Instead of telling yourself you must not forget something, tell yourself that you must remember it. If you start off worrying that you might forget something, the chances are you will!

→ **Mind Map.** Mind Maps, of course, are an easy way to get your imagination on board and help you remember things. This is because they naturally engage the right side of your brain with their use of colour and image.

→ **Image** plays a major part of your recall, encapsulated in the saying, 'a picture is worth a thousand words.' A Mind Map is not only a picture but a picture that contains pictures.

Each of the above techniques can be used to great advantage on your Mind Maps to help you remember the information you add to them. Mind Maps are not just the ultimate thinking tool – they are also the ultimate memory tool.

# The Power of Association

Looking for associations between ideas or information helps your brain to make links between them and encourages it to think synergetically. In a synergetic system, 1 + 1 will equal more than 2, i.e. if you can link something you want to learn to something you already know, you will not only find it easier to remember the new idea, but you will also broaden your understanding of the original idea and/or arrive at a new understanding. For example, let's say that you are learning about the planets in our universe for the first time. You are given the following pieces of information:

1.  There are nine planets in our solar system.

2.  In the correct order from the Sun, the planets are: Mercury, Venus, Earth, Mars, Jupiter, Saturn, Uranus, Neptune, Pluto.

3.  Mercury, Venus, Earth, and Mars are small planets; Jupiter, Saturn, Uranus, and Neptune are large planets; and Pluto is a small planet.

4.  The larger a planet is, the stronger its gravitational pull.

5.  The closer the planets are to the Sun, the more light and heat reaches them.

Having learnt these five pieces of information you later overhear a conversation between two people on a bus. They are speculating about the possibility of life on Neptune. Because your brain thinks synergetically you find that you can contribute intelligently to this conversation: in order for life to be sustained it would need to be on a planet that provides light, warmth, oxygen, and a moderate gravitational pull. You know that Neptune is far away from the Sun, which means that there would be little light and warmth. You also know that

Neptune is a large planet so its gravitational pull will be immense – far stronger than most life forms could support. From this you can conclude – even though you don't know if Neptune can provide oxygen – that it is highly unlikely that there is life on Neptune.

Mind Maps help your brain to make associations and great leaps of understanding. They multiply your brain's core activity to make connections.

## Help Your Brain Make Associations

When you want to memorize something, help your brain make associations by looking for or using:

→ **Patterns**. Always look for patterns in information you want to remember. For example, if you are going to the supermarket and need to remember which groceries to buy, organize your food stuffs in groups (fruit, vegetables, meat, and so on). Other patterns you can look for include order of size, order of events, and groups of colour. The way you draw a Mind Map automatically helps you identify patterns in information.

→ **Numbers**. Numbering information in order can really help you remember lists of facts.

→ **Symbols**. Using symbols and pictures is an excellent way of creating triggers for your memory. For example, every time you come up with a particularly good idea you can draw a light bulb beside it.

→ **Mind Maps**. The art of drawing Mind Maps encourages your brain to make associations: each branch links one thought to another. Mind Maps are also a brilliant way of organizing information in groups on a page and using images as trigger symbols.

# Memorizing Information from a Mind Map

The simple act of Mind Mapping what you want to remember, whether it is a collection of facts, a speech, or words and rules for a foreign language, will naturally help you to memorize it. This is because, as we have already observed, Mind Maps are so good at getting you to use imagination and association. However, there are ways you can use your Mind Maps for studying that will help you retain the information on them. The most important of these is how often you review them.

# Repetition and Memory

There is a specific formula for how often you should go over information in order to fix it in your long-term memory. This is as follows:

| | |
|---|---|
| **1st review** | Just after you first learnt it |
| **2nd review** | One day after you first learnt it |
| **3rd review** | One week after you first learnt it |
| **4th review** | One month after you first learnt it |
| **5th review** | Three to six months after you first learn it |

If you follow this formula you will permanently memorize what you want to learn – and even start to remember more as your brain will be thinking synergetically about the information it stores and start to make new links between what it knows.

# The Importance of Study Breaks

You will also find it easier to retain information if you take regular breaks between each study period. During breaks your brain will be integrating what it has learnt naturally and spontaneously building up internal Mind Maps of thought.

You also need to take breaks because your brain finds it easier to remember more from the start and end of a study period than it does in the middle. When you take regular breaks the amount of time in the middle of your study session is reduced and there is less information at risk of being lost in the middle.

Ideally, each study session should last about 45 minutes before you give yourself a 5- or 10-minute break. Go out of the room and think about something else, step out in the fresh air and move around. Whilst you are relaxing your brain will actually be quite busy: it will be sorting through and filing the information you have given it. When you return to your studies, your brain will feel refreshed and you will also find it easier to concentrate.

## The natural study tool

**When you draw a Mind Map you are constantly seeing in your peripheral vision what you have already done whilst working on a new area. Mind Maps allow you to work on new material whilst automatically reviewing the rest of your Mind Map.**

# Top 10 Creativity Tips

✔  1.  **MIND MAP**

Use Mind Maps whenever you have a creative problem you wish to explore. Do it in the following stages:

➜ Draw a quick Mind Map of what you want to brainstorm, adding colour, images, and as much information as your brain wishes. This exercise should be done at high speed.

➜ Let your brain 'think on it' for a while, giving yourself at least an hour's break.

➜ Return to the Mind Map and add any new thoughts you have had.

➜ Look at your Mind Map closely again, finding any new connections you can between any of the elements on any of the branches.

➜ Connect these elements by codes, colours, or arrows.

➜ Identify the main new connections.

➜ Take another break to allow your brain to think on it again.

➜ Look at your Mind Map again, and identify and mark any new connections you can now see.

➜ Return to the Mind Map and decide on your solution!

### ✔ 2. USE COLOUR IN YOUR NOTES

Always use colour in your notes – preferably as part of a Mind Map as colour is a major feature. Start off with a four-colour ballpoint pen, and move on to other colours as you progress. Colour makes your notes more interesting; it will stimulate your creative-thinking processes, and will, literally, add colour to your life!

### ✔ 3. DAYDREAM AND NIGHTDREAM!

Both daydreaming and nightdreaming give your visual creative muscles added strength. Note, preferably in Mind Map form, any ideas or images from your best dreams. This will encourage you to be more visual and colourful in your Mind Mapping notes.

### ✔ 4. THINK RADIANTLY

Once a week, take any word or concept that interests you, and play a creative game with yourself like the coat-hanger game to help your radiant thinking skills. This will keep your Mind Mapping skills in shape.

### ✔ 5. KEEP MIND MAP NOTEBOOKS

Another great creative genius who made visual Mind Map-type notes was Thomas Edison, and he did so because Leonardo da Vinci had!

Edison, who filed patent after patent after patent with the US authorities, was driven by a burning creative desire, and decided that the best way to fuel his own creative genius would be to follow in the footsteps of his hero Leonardo. Following Leonardo's example, Edison studiously and passionately recorded, with visual illustrations, every step of his creative-thinking processes, and eventually amassed 3,500 notebooks.

✔  6.    **USE MIND MAPS AS A CREATIVE COMMUNICATION TOOL**

If you have to make a speech or talk of any sort, use a Creative Mind Map to help guarantee a successful presentation of your ideas.

Regardless of whether your speech is a short thank-you speech after a dinner or celebration, or a full-blown formal business presentation, a creative Mind Map has a number of advantages over the standard and normal linear, boring, monotonous, pre-prepared, often humourless presentations that make many people afraid to speak in public, and audiences to dread such events too!

By using a Mind Map you can organize your thoughts quickly, put them in an appropriate order, and include all the key ideas and images that will spark your imagination when you get up to speak. This will help you to relax and talk naturally and spontaneously – to the relief and enjoyment of everyone concerned!

✔  7.    **MIND MAP AND CREATE YOUR FUTURE**

For this exercise, place an image or symbol of yourself in the centre of your Mind Map and have as your main branches such topics as Skills; Education; Travel; Family; Job; Wealth; Health; Friends; Goals; Hobbies. On this Mind Map create your ideal future – Mind-Mapping the rest of your life as you would design it if a genie from the magic lamp had granted your every wish (see also Chapter Six).

When you have created this ideal future Mind Map, set about making it come true. Many people have tried this 'create your own life' Mind Map approach and have found it to be extraordinarily successful. Within a few years of creating their Mind Maps they have found that as much as 80 percent of their plans have been accomplished!

✔  8.   **MAKE AN IMAGE-ONLY MIND MAP**

Make a Mind Map using only images – no words at all! Your brain will make different connections and associations when it is dealing only with images. You may be quite surprised at the new creative links and connections you make when you explore a topic in this way.

✔  9.   **COLOUR-CODE YOUR MIND MAPS**

Find four ways to use colour as a code in your Mind Maps. Build up ways that you can use colour and/or texture to show connections, layers of time or thought, people, actions, urgency, etc.

✔  10.   **EXPLORE HOW USING MIND MAPS CAN HELP YOU IN YOUR LIFE**

Mind Map all the ways Mind Maps can assist you – at home, at work, in all areas of your life. Keep building and extending this Mind Map. Add others' ideas on to yours as well! Study carefully the Mind Map on p. 139 that sums up all the creativity tips above. Use it as a check list to help you develop your creative skills.

# Creativity Is the Key to Mental Success

Creativity is the key to your mental success, both in terms of coming up with startling and original ideas, and in terms of memorizing whatever you want. Your brain is naturally creative and you need only to provide it with the right environment to unlock its full creative potential. Nurture every opportunity you have to be creative, always try to be flexible and to get away from the norm – believe that your ideas, like your brain, are truly exceptional – and remember that Mind Maps are your greatest ally when it comes to releasing your genius within.

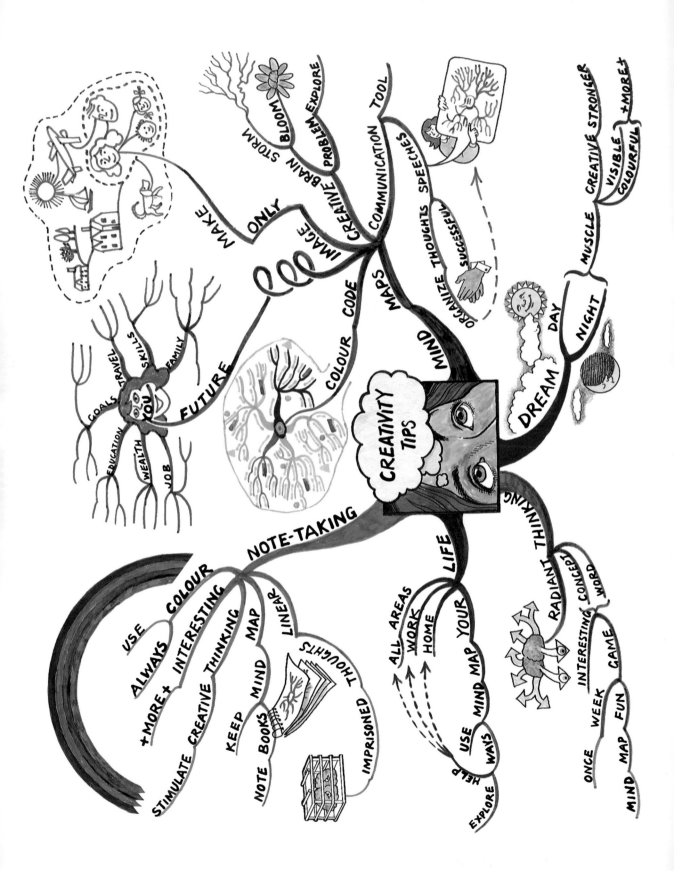

# Physical Fitness for Mental Power

*A definite relationship has been found between physical fitness and mental alertness and emotional stability ... improved endurance performance makes the body less susceptible to fatigue, and consequently less likely to commit errors, mental or physical.*

Dr Kenneth Cooper, United States Air Force School of Aerospace Medicine

# Overview of
# Chapter 5:

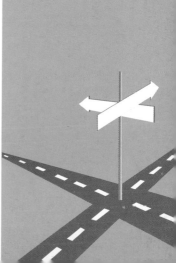

You may not realize it but if you want your mind to function at its peak, you need to nurture it physically as well as mentally. This means a superb diet, balanced amounts of sleep and relaxation, and a proper level of fitness. Your brain works in absolute integration with your incredible body: to be mentally fit you have to look after your body, and to be physically fit, you also have to look after your brain.

This chapter explores the best ways of keeping your Mind Map-making brain cells in tip-top condition. It will also give you guidelines on how best to nurture your body to harness your mental power – with the help of Mind Maps.

## Quick Brain-check

Most people know that a good fitness and lifestyle routine will improve their physical health, giving them stronger muscles, a healthy heart, and reducing their risk of getting diseases like cancer and diabetes. But do you think that by becoming more healthy you will:

1. Experience giant leaps in self-confidence, self-respect, and self-empowerment **YES/NO?**

2. Attract more people to you **YES/NO?**

3. Improve general relationships **YES/NO?**

4. Gain respect from family, friends, colleagues and people at large **YES/NO?**

5. Increase your probability of getting a better job **YES/NO?**

6. Reduce mental stress and tension **YES/NO?**

Extraordinarily, all these claims are true!

# The New Science of Body and Mind

Research and psychological and medical health findings confirm that people who are physically active score better across-the-board on all tests of mental skills than those who are unfit. If you test your mental skills when you are unfit, and then test them again, after having become very fit, you will find a significant overall improvement.

Similarly research has confirmed that the reverse of this is also true. The child who, in general, scores better in tests of mental skills is, on average, fitter, healthier, and more emotionally well-adjusted and happy than the child whose mental skills test results are poor.

Your body is the bastion, the protector, the transportation system, the nourisher, and the provider for your brain. Maintain it, and it will maintain you. Neglect and abuse it, and you simply neglect and abuse your magical self.

The Mind Map on the following page, The Body's Major Systems, offers an overview of the miracle that is your body.

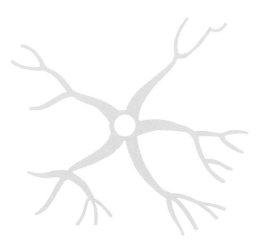

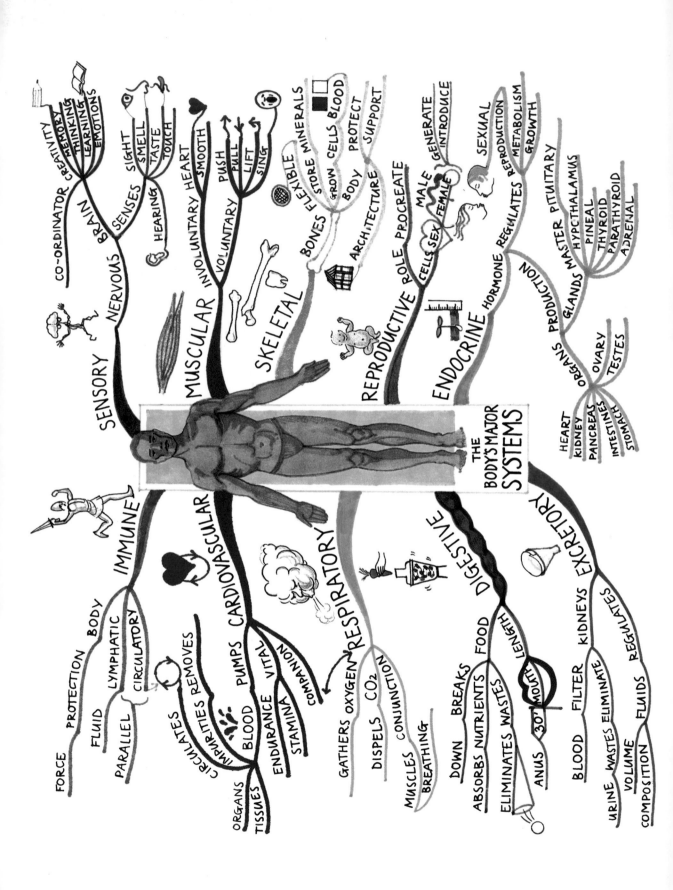

THE BODY'S MAJOR SYSTEMS

SENSORY / NERVOUS
- CO-ORDINATOR
- BRAIN
  - CREATIVITY
  - MEMORY
  - THINKING
  - LEARNING
  - EMOTIONS
- SENSES
  - SIGHT
  - SMELL
  - TASTE
  - TOUCH
  - HEARING

MUSCULAR
- INVOLUNTARY HEART
  - SMOOTH
- VOLUNTARY
  - PUSH
  - PULL
  - LIFT
  - SING

SKELETAL
- BONES
  - FLEXIBLE
  - STORE MINERALS
  - GROW CELLS BLOOD
  - BODY PROTECT SUPPORT
  - ARCHITECTURE

REPRODUCTIVE
- ROLE PROCREATE
- CELLS
  - MALE
  - SEX FEMALE
  - GENERATE
  - INTRODUCE
- SEXUAL
  - REPRODUCTION
  - REGULATES

ENDOCRINE
- HORMONE REGULATES
  - METABOLISM
  - GROWTH
- PRODUCTION
- GLANDS MASTER PITUITARY
  - HYPOTHALAMUS
  - PINEAL
  - THYROID
  - PARATHYROID
  - ADRENAL
- ORGANS
  - OVARY
  - TESTES
  - HEART
  - KIDNEY
  - PANCREAS
  - INTESTINES
  - STOMACH

IMMUNE
- PROTECTION BODY
- FLUID LYMPHATIC
  - PARALLEL CIRCULATORY
  - FORCE
  - IMPURITIES REMOVES
  - CIRCULATES
  - ORGANS
  - TISSUES

CARDIOVASCULAR
- PUMPS
  - BLOOD
- VITAL
  - ENDURANCE
  - STAMINA
- COMPANION

RESPIRATORY
- GATHERS OXYGEN
- DISPELS CO₂
- CONJUNCTION
  - MUSCLES
  - BREATHING

DIGESTIVE
- FOOD BREAKS DOWN
- ABSORBS NUTRIENTS
- ELIMINATES WASTES
- LENGTH MOUTH 30'
- ANUS

EXCRETORY
- KIDNEYS FILTER
  - BLOOD
- WASTES ELIMINATE
  - URINE
- REGULATES FLUIDS
  - VOLUME
  - COMPOSITION

# Myth-busting

**MYTH:**  'Bright people (nerds) are unfit; fit people are thick!'

**TRUTH:**  If you exercise your brain (particularly with the help of Mind Maps) you will positively influence your body; if you exercise your body you will positively influence your brain.
Remember: The bright are strong and the strong are brighter!

**MYTH:**  'Pure aerobics is all you need to stay fit.'

**TRUTH:**  Yes, you do need aerobics. But you also need Poise, Flexibility and Strength if you are to be truly fit.

**MYTH:**  'If you exercise you don't have to be so concerned with what you eat.'

**TRUTH:**  When you exercise you need to be even more concerned with what you eat. This is a simple and obvious one. When you exercise, you are placing more demands on your body than normal. If your body is having demands placed on it, it needs to be completely prepared to meet those energy demands. If your nutrition is inadequate, then the body will not be able to respond to the exercise challenge, and in this depleted state will place itself at risk of damage or injury. A good well-rounded diet is essential if you are to exercise well and to your maximum benefit.

# General Physical Fitness

To become an Olympic *mental* athlete you need to work on four main areas of *physical* fitness:

1. **Poise**

2. **Aerobic training and fitness**

3. **Flexibility**

4. **Strength**

## 1. PERFECT POISE FOR FLUID THINKING

Poise is important! It is the perfect balance of the body, in which all aspects of your muscular, organic, and skeletal systems are properly aligned. Of particular importance are the relative positioning of your head, neck, spine, and joints. It is possible to be aerobically, flexibly, and muscularly fit, yet still to be 'off balance'. This is why poise forms the first column in your temple of general physical fitness for mental power.

### Posture Power

If you think about extreme cases, the importance of poise becomes blazingly obvious. If you are sitting, as many people do, for over six hours a day in a slouched and badly aligned position, just think about what happens to your amazing body:

→ All your internal organs get squashed and cramped into a massively restricted space. This directly, immediately, and negatively affects their vital functioning, to keep your body balanced and powerful.

→ Your lung capacity will be significantly reduced. This will force you to take short, gasping breaths, thus supplying less vital oxygen to your body and, particularly, to your Mind Map-generating brain.

→ Your cardiovascular system. In a slouched position most of your major arteries and blood vessels will be constricted. It is as if you were putting multiple clamps on all the major 'tubes' of your blood supply system. This also puts an extra strain and tension on your heart, which has to pump harder in order to force your blood through.

→ Your nerves. As with the blood, a cramped and slouched posture pinches the nerves, slowing down the transmission of essential 'Nerve Knowledge' and often causing pain in the process.

→ Your muscles have to work much harder to keep you in position if your balance is 'off kilter'.

Equally, if your body is off balance when you are involved in any aerobic activity, then discomfort and injury will be the probable eventual outcomes. Obviously, exactly the same is true for any muscular lifting, pulling or pushing activity, or weight training.

Nor do you have to be very active for inappropriate poise to cause serious injury – standing in high heels is one example! Being forced into this unnatural position can tip the pelvis, spine, back, and knees out of alignment and can, over time, seriously damage your musculo-skeletal system.

Bad posture                     Good posture

Proper poise allows fluidity of movement, and a natural flow of all your mental and physical energies. This is often described as a 'balanced resting state', in which the body, no matter what its position, is fundamentally alert and ready to spring effectively into action from non-action, and into other action from any existing action. One of the best examples of this is a cat.

## Keep Your Poise in Mind

Develop an appropriate awareness of the relative excellence of your poise in your everyday activities such as walking, running, sitting down, standing up, bending, lifting, eating, brushing your teeth, talking on the telephone, listening, driving the car, and especially during all forms of physical exercise. Run through in your mind the following checklist:

→ Am I slouching?

→ Am I stiffening my neck?

→ Am I pulling my head back/slumping it forward?

→ Am I raising my shoulders unnecessarily?

→ Am I locking any joints?

→ Am I thrusting my hips forward and the small of my back inward?

→ Is my breathing deep, free, and rhythmical or shallow, gasping, and 'held'?

## Use the Success Formula TEFCAS to Improve Your Posture

Stand in front of a mirror, and simply look at the creature in front of you. Objectively, 'Check' what you see. Is your head perfectly aligned or is it tilted in any direction on top of your spine? Is one shoulder higher than the other (in most people one is)? Do your arms hang by your sides evenly? Are any of your joints 'locked'?

When your senses have received this 'Feedback' and your brain has 'Checked', pause, and allow your natural 'Perfect Poise' to reintroduce itself.

Alternatively, consider taking up a 'good poise' hobby that encourages good poise. Excellent disciplines for helping you to attain poise include certain forms of dance and yoga, the Japanese martial art of Aikido, and, especially, the Alexander Technique.

## 2. AEROBIC EXERCISE FOR THE MIND

At the beginning of the 21st century 14,000 children aged between 8 and 12 participated in a study to trace the effects of exercise on academic performance. The study concluded that those pupils who do regular exercise do better in the 'three R's'. Those who took part in a sport or vigorous activity three times a week were more likely to get good scores in their examinations.

One of the findings of the study, for example, found that 79 percent of boys who scored above average marks in national English tests also exercised at least three times a week. Of those children who scored below average, only 38 percent exercised for the same period.

The scientist who led the study, Angela Balding, said:

*'There's a definite link between those who are active three or four times a week and those youngsters who do better in the classroom. The research that is going into brain activity at the moment suggests that the reason may be that in those kids who are active, more oxygen gets to their brains. Their brains are then better equipped to take more in and be receptive to new things.'*

Aerobics exercise is any exercise that stimulates heart and lung activity for a time period sufficiently long to produce significant and beneficial changes in the body. Typical aerobic exercises include fast walking, running, swimming, cycling, and rowing.

Aerobic training builds up your stamina and endurance by forcing your heart to pump more life-giving and oxygen-carrying blood to all the muscles and organs of your body – including your brain.

Aerobic fitness is an overall fitness often called 'endurance fitness' or 'working capacity' – your ability to do prolonged work without undue fatigue.

Aerobic exercise specifically produces a training effect that increases the ability of your body to utilize oxygen.

→ It improves the size, strength, and pumping efficiency of your heart. This means that with each beat, more blood can be pumped around your body.

→ This improves your ability to transport life-sustaining oxygen from your lungs to your heart and ultimately to all other parts of your body.

→ It strengthens your breathing muscles. This tends to reduce the resistance to air flow, making breathing easier, and ultimately facilitates the rapid flow of air in and out of your lungs.

→ It tones up the muscles throughout your body. This improves your general circulation, can lower your blood pressure, and reduces the workload on your heart.

→ It produces an increase in the total amount of blood circulating in your body and makes your blood a more efficient oxygen carrier.

→ It feeds your brain with more oxygen, helping your brain cells to create more powerful Mind Map thought patterns.

In summary, aerobic training exercises the inside of your body that needs to be fit, by increasing the body's ability to take in one of its main 'fuels' – oxygen.

## Exercise Exercises Your Brain

Research has confirmed the positive relationship between exercise and mental performance. In 2001 Dr James Blumenthal and his colleagues at Duke University Medical Center in North Carolina computed that half-an-hour of aerobic activity three times a week was sufficient to bring about a significant increase in brainpower. In the experiment, it was confirmed that such exercise can boost memory and can help combat the effects of aging. Indeed, the improvements in mental and general performance were especially marked for the middle-aged and elderly. The improvements in performance were both immediate and long-lasting.

### The Correct Aerobic Formula

To become and stay aerobically fit (oxygen fit) you need to exercise four times a week, for a minimum of 30 minutes a time.

Forms of exercise that particularly help you become aerobically fit, and which, when you do them well, are extremely enjoyable and satisfying, include swimming, fast and long-distance walking, running, cross-country skiing, dancing, rowing, making love, and using the growing range of aerobic training machines that mimic a number of these activities.

Each exercise session should start with a five-minute warm-up, followed by 20 minutes of hard aerobic fitness training, followed by a five-minute cool-down and stretching period. The warm-up period ensures that your body will be 'revved up' for the exercise to come. The cool-down period guarantees a smooth transition between hard exercise and your normal activity.

When you maintain hard aerobic training for at least 20 minutes, a message is sent to your brain and body that they are in danger of running out of oxygen. This is life threatening! As a result, a 'red alert' message goes out to all systems, instructing them to 'crank up' in order to deal with the increased demands. This is why doing the activity for at least 20 minutes is so vital. If you train for only 10–15 minutes per session, your brain and body will say to themselves something like 'Oh, this is a little bit difficult, but it's not going to last for long. No need to change.'

It is this phenomenal ability of your system to adjust itself to the stresses and strains being placed on it that is the basis of aerobic training, and as you will see in the strength-building section of this chapter, muscular development training too.

During the time of hard aerobic training, your heart should maintain a pulse rate of between 120 and 180 beats per minute (depending upon your age and current physical condition).

The effects of even this modest amount of exercise on your body and brain are astonishing.

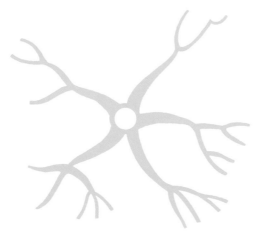

# A Body Workout is a Brain Workout

Rodney Swain and his colleagues at the University of Wisconsin in Milwaukee have come up with some remarkable findings about the speed with which the brain adapts positively to exercise, regardless of age.

Studies had previously shown that young animals sprout blood vessels in the brain after bursts of exercise. The suspicion was that this was only possible early in life. To test the truth of this, Swain and his colleagues tested middle-aged rats, some of whom did, and some of whom didn't do 'rat aerobics'.

The rats that declined to take exercise showed no change in their brains. The rats that had done aerobics showed a dramatic increase in the density of blood vessels in the regions of their brains connected to exercise. The astonishing thing about this finding was that 'all the growth had taken place within three days of initiating aerobic activity,' Swain said. 'It shows that the brain can make rapid changes to its oxygen supply'.

Swain suggests that because the neurons in the brain are stepping up activity in conjunction with the exercise, they need more nutrients and oxygen. Noting this need, the brain uses the extra energy from the aerobic exercise to sprout extra capillaries to supply the extra nutrients and oxygen in the newly working areas of the brain.

Interestingly, Swain speculates that cognitive workouts (thinking and Mind Sport activities) will probably also encourage the formation of new blood vessels to the 'thinking areas' of the brain.

Encouragingly, the animals who had shown this increase also, of choice, began to run up to three times further each day, suggesting that the brain and the body were both cooperating in guaranteeing the supply of more of this new 'drug' – **healthy blood!**

## The Effect of Aerobics on Your Brain

The prime beneficiary of your aerobic fitness is your brain – *mens sana in corpore sano*, a healthy mind in a healthy body! When your body is fit, your brain performs better too.

With every beat of your heart, blood is pumped directly into your brain. Bearing in mind the fact that your brain weighs only between 2 and 3 percent of your body weight, and that many of the capillaries that carry blood to it are microscopically small, a whopping 20–40 percent of the blood goes directly into your brain with every beat of your heart!

Nature considers your brain to be by far the most important part of you.

Aerobic exercise will increase the quality of your sleep and will often lessen the amount you require. When you are aerobically fit you give your brain a deeper and more meaningful rest and integrating period for one quarter to one third of every day. The remaining 66–75 percent of the day is then spent in a state of higher sensory and intellectual alertness and awareness.

## The Psychological Effects of Aerobic Training

Because of the intimate connection between the brain and body, physical fitness can now be seen to be in many ways equivalent to mental fitness.

Tests have shown highly positive correlations between performances in physical tests and exercises, and academic and leadership qualities. They have also revealed a positive correlation between physical health and mental outlook. People who are in good aerobic condition tend to be more self-confident, more optimistic, more determined, and generally have a greater love of their jobs and professions, a generally higher energy level, and a greater lust for life.

# 3. FLEXIBLE BODY, FLEXIBLE MIND

Flexibility fitness refers to the ability of your body's joints to move freely in all the directions for which they were designed. For a masterful demonstration of just how flexible your joints can be, just watch any baby.

When your body is flexible your muscles are able to extend to their full length, thus keeping them supple and avoiding the danger of damage to both them and your skeleton.

Your nervous system is also able to send its messages more smoothly to any part of your body without being pinched or blocked by areas of muscular rigidity and tension. Similarly oxygen can flow more freely through the joints, blood vessels, and capillaries when your body is more open.

Flexibility is a deep-rooted and basic need. This is demonstrated in the stretch reflex – that frequent desire of ourselves and animals to have a good yawn or stretch. Stretching in all directions is one of the best flexibility exercises there is, and can be naturally and easily performed on a daily basis. Again, one of the best instructors in this area of physical fitness is the cat.

Always ensure that whenever you are doing any aerobic or strength training, you include flexibility exercises as part of your warm-up and cool-down. Other exercises that are specifically designed to increase flexibility include dance, yoga, gymnastics, Aikido, and aerobic 'stretchercizes'.

When your body is flexible, so is your mind – creative ideas will flow from that fantastic brain of yours particularly if you use Mind Maps, the ultimate flexible thinking tool.

# 4. STRENGTHEN YOUR BODY TO STRENGTHEN YOUR MIND MAPS OF THOUGHT

Muscular strength is an important part of your overall health. It refers to the ability of all your muscles and muscle systems to lift, pull, push, and rotate. When you are strong in body you are strong in mind.

Strength training has a number of advantages:

➡ It tones up your muscles.

➡ It strengthens your bones.

➡ It allows greater general functional ability.

➡ It gives you more power to perform any of the physical tasks in your everyday life.

➡ It provides a solid basis for any sporting/athletic activity.

➡ It lessens your chance of injury.

➡ It helps protect your internal organs.

➡ It increases self-confidence.

➡ It makes you look good.

➡ It makes you feel good!

## The Muscle Building for a Strong Mind

Ideally you need to take muscle-building exercise four times a week for 20–60 minutes, depending upon the number of muscles and muscle groups you wish to strengthen.

## Super All-round Exercises

If you are wondering how to find the time to work aerobically, build flexibility and strength, AND improve your posture, don't! There are forms of exercise that you can do that combine all four. These are also all ways to help strengthen the Mind Maps of your mind.

## Swimming

Swimming is one of the best all-round exercises there is. It provides you with automatic aerobic training, helps to develop flexibility, and it encourages muscular development, especially when you do regular sprinting sessions in the pool – the equivalent of 'Water Weight-Training'! Swimming has the added advantage of being 'non-impact' and therefore dramatically reduces the chance of physical stress-related injuries.

## Running

Running shares many of the advantages of swimming, in that it exercises all the muscles in your body, naturally incorporates aerobic training, and develops muscular strength as well. It is especially important in running to have excellent poise, as this massively decreases the chance of injury.

The advantage that running has over swimming is that you are 'competing' with gravity; you therefore use more energy per unit time. The disadvantage of this is, however, is that it involves your body in continuous impact with the ground.

Running will make you slimmer and leaner and 'thinner', but if you want to incorporate muscle building into your running program, include regular and consistent sprint training.

## Walking

To be a good all-round training exercise, walking needs to be fast! When it is, it becomes virtually identical to running – the main differences being that it uses slightly less energy per minute, and it involves far less impact on your joints, and therefore less chance of injury to ankles, knees, and hips.

## Rowing

Rowing requires extreme aerobic fitness, and obviously at the same time demands that the body be flexible and extremely muscularly powerful. Poise is also a major factor, in that a well-balanced head significantly increases the pushing and pulling power of the athlete.

Rowing ergometers are now among the most popular general exercise machines, and are highly commended. As with running and swimming, rowing exercises all of your main muscle groups and, like swimming, it is a non-impact exercise and therefore reduces your risk of injury during training.

## Dancing

Dancing, especially salsa, Latin, free, jazz, and classical, is both a natural desire and one of the best all-round exercises there is, especially when you incorporate many different moves. Dancing encourages excellent poise, requires considerable muscular strength, especially in any lifting or throwing routines with partners, is one of the best methods of acquiring flexibility, and is similarly one of the best aerobic training sports when it is maintained at a high pace, non-stop, for periods of more than 20 minutes at a time.

It is also fun, making you happier, reducing your stress levels, and involving and opening up your senses.

The table below shows the calories you can burn per minute in a number of standard physical and athletic exercises:

| Activity | Calories Expended per Minute |
|---|---|
| Walking 2 mph | 2.8 |
| Walking 3.5 mph | 4.8 |
| Cycling 5.5 mph | 3.2 |
| Cycling rapidly | 6.9 |
| Running 5.7 mph | 12.0 |
| Running 7.0 mph | 14.5 |
| Running 11.4 mph | 21.7 |
| Swimming (crawl) 2.2 mph | 26.7 |
| Swimming (breaststroke) 2.2 mph | 30.8 |
| Swimming (backstroke) 2.2 mph | 33.3 |
| Golf | 5.0 |
| Tennis | 7.1 |
| Table tennis | 5.8 |
| Dancing (foxtrot) | 5.2 |

The average man requires only 1,500 calories a day, whereas the average woman requires only 1,200. The table below shows how little food you actually need to consume in order to provide your body with its minimum requirement of 1,500 calories per day. Eat with intelligence and you'll become more intelligent!

Food portions that provide you with 100 calories:

| Amount | Foodstuff |
| --- | --- |
| 1 | cup of orange juice |
| 5 | fresh apricots |
| ½ cup | cup of rice |
| ⅓ cup | spaghetti with tomato sauce |
| 1½ cups | strawberries |
| 15 | almonds |
| 1 | big apple |
| ⅓ cup | baked beans |
| 8oz | beer |
| 1oz | Cheddar cheese |
| 1 | grapefruit |
| 1 | honeydew melon |
| 1 | lettuce |
| 1 cup | coffee with cream and sugar |
| 1 | pancake |
| ½ cup | cereal |
| 2 tbsp | sugar |
| 1 | fried egg |
| 5oz | glass of milk |
| ½ cup | tinned tuna |
| ½ cup | tomato or vegetable soup |
| 8oz | glass of soft drink |
| ⅔ oz | chocolate |
| 1 oz | whisky |
| 2 oz | minced beef |
| 1 | baked potato |
| 6 | crisps |
| 5 | fries |
| 1½ | apples |
| 1 scoop | ice cream |
| 2 | plain biscuits |

# A Physical Star

Not long ago Ian Thorpe was a 'dumpy little kid' who was so uncoordinated at ball games that he was everyone's last pick for their team. His father, who worked for a local council in Sydney sweeping leaves, reported that the boy was also allergic to chlorine!

Hardly the right ingredients for a boy who was to become the greatest swimmer of all time.

Within 10 years this kid had:

→ become the youngest male swimmer ever to represent Australia

→ become the youngest male world champion at the World Championships

→ broken four world records in four days at the age of 16

→ broken 22 Olympic and World Records by the age of 19

→ been voted the 'World's Most Outstanding Athlete'

*How did he do it?*

**Answer:** by having a clear personal vision of winning gold medals, by having a stated ambition in life 'to be the best I can be', by making sure that 'all his systems *can* go!' and by focussing on the balance between his body and mind and his sport and life.

# Ian Thorpe, the Thorpedo

Ian's dedication is absolute. His training consists of 10 sessions a week, 5 in the morning and 5 in the afternoon. His day starts with his alarm set to go off at 4.17 am in order to be in the pool by 5.00 am. In addition to these 10 sessions, Ian adds 2 weight-training and 2 aerobic-based stamina-enhancing boxing sessions.

As well as his rigorous training, the Thorpedo spends a lot of time working with his charity devoted to developing the body, mind, and spirit of children around the world, as well as helping people find ways to fight cancer.

Described by his coaches as an avid learner, a flexible thinker, and a highly intelligent and well-rounded individual, the Thorpedo lives by the philosophy that you should be passionate about and love everything that you do.

So great is his energy that in the pool the men who trail him (which is nearly everyone!) say that it's like being immersed in a washing machine!

Ian's charity work and love for humanity extends to his prime life goal after swimming: to work for the United Nations. His reputation for honesty and moral certainty will stand him in good stead. Sue Mott, sports columnist for the *Daily Telegraph*, said:

*'Thorpe is the real thing, the embodiment of a gracious, charismatic champion.'*

# DID YOU KNOW THAT ...?

→ You have 200 intricately architectured bones, 500 totally coordinated muscles, and 7 miles of nerve fibers to move your body?

→ Within your body there is enough atomic energy to build any of the world's greatest cities many times over?

→ Your heart beats on average 36 million times every year, pumping 600,000 gallons of blood through 60,000 miles of arteries, veins, and capillaries?

→ The blood circulating in the human body contains 22 trillion blood cells? Within each blood cell are millions of molecules, and within each molecule is an atom oscillating at more than 10 million times per second.

→ Two million blood cells die each second? These are immediately replaced with two million more!

→ The human olfactory system can identify the chemical odorant of an object in one part per trillion of air?

→ Throughout the human body there are 500,000 touch sensors?

→ Your mouth is the most sophisticated chemical laboratory the planet has ever known? It can distinguish, by using combinations of sweet, sour, salt, and bitter taste sensations as well as odour, over a billion different tastes.

→ In short, you are a walking miracle!

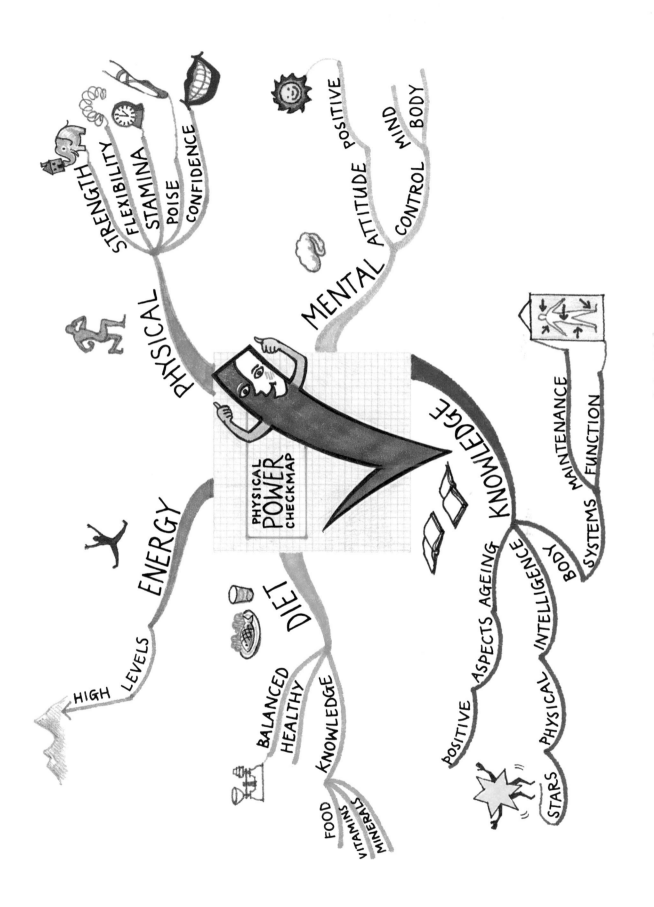

# A Mind Against All Odds

Imagine that as a young man at the age of 26, you are told that you have cancer. Not a mild cancer, but one that started in your testicles, spread to your abdomen, then to your lungs, and finally to your brain.

Imagine then that you were told you had less than a 20 per cent chance of surviving (and this is an optimistic assessment!), that you had to undergo months of chemotherapy and radiotherapy, and, in addition, that you had to have your brain operated on to extract the vicious tumour.

Imagine then that you are asked if you would mind competing, in less than 2 years' time, in 20 marathon races spread over 24 days. Not only *that*, but you are expected to win the overall total of all those marathons. And not only that – you are expected to do this for 6 years in a row.

Someone did have all those cancers and someone did ask that someone to compete in those marathons. The person who had the cancers was Lance Armstrong; the person who asked him to compete and win was himself! And he did!

Lance Armstrong has won 6 consecutive Tour de France bike races in which the riders race for 20 days over distances that often exceed 200 km. Some days the races are on the flat. Some days the races are up the steepest mountains in the Alps and Pyrenees. Sometimes the races are against the clock. In each type of terrain, there is usually a group of specialists. Lance Armstrong has won them all! *How* did he do it?

By mind over matter, by incredible acts of will, by a phenomenal all-round physical-training program, and by acquiring a complete knowledge of his body and its dietary and psychological needs. In so doing he built up one of the most phenomenal immune systems the world has ever known. In trying to explain why Armstrong was so dominant, the *Herald Tribune* once noted:

*'A combination of speed and power may be enough to win the Tour de France, as many riders have proven, once. To prove it 4 times, a rider needs to add focus, consistency, dedication … and health. Of these, dedication might be the foremost. Asked recently when he would begin preparing for the next season (after having just won the Tour de France), Armstrong replied, "I've already started."'*

Lance's attitude towards failure or defeat is to learn from it and then to excel. Lance's Director Sportif, Johan Bruyneel, likes to tell the story of Lance's training rides on the Joux Plan, an Alpine climb where Armstrong faltered on his way to overall victory in 2000, the only bad day he has had in the last 6 Tours de France. Although the Joux Plan was not on the itinerary for 2002, Armstrong was training there in the spring, working on conquering his conqueror. He rode up it once, turned around at the peak, barrelled down and climbed it again. That day he spent 8 hours in the saddle, suffering terrible fatigue. A few days later, Armstrong won the Joux Plan stage in the Dauphine Libere Race!

It is no coincidence that Lance is never interested in resting on his laurels – he is always trying to strive for improvement. He uses Michael Schumacher's sport as a metaphor: 'We take a Formula One approach. Formula One teams are always testing, always tinkering. Testing the brakes, testing the tires, testing the engine, always trying to improve. That's us, too.'

Lance's whole attitude can be summed up by the fact that when he was first told of his serious cancers, he decided, despite the tiny probability of his living, to label himself, not as a cancer victim, but rather as a 'cancer survivor'.

Using the awesome strength of his mental powers he has held that monster at bay for 8 years and accomplished physical feats which, in the context of his health history, are miraculous.

# Feed Your Body, Feed Your Mind

Does the quality of the food you eat make a difference to your physical health and, most importantly, your brain-power? Yes it does, and there is increasing evidence to support this. What you feed your body is just as important as how trim you keep it when it comes to peak mental performance.

## Diet and IQ

A study was undertaken at the University of Auckland Psychology Clinic and involved 16 cases of children classified as minimally brain-damaged, hyperactive or slow learners. In all cases, their diets were adjusted to reduce the levels of toxic metals in their bodies, eliminate allergies, and to diminish the amount of processed foods, soft drinks, and sweets they ate.

As Dr Colgan reported: 'Over periods from three to six months, every case showed improvements in behaviour, at home, at school and in the clinic, as well as in motor co-ordination, speech articulation and reading skills.'

What Dr. Colgan did not expect was perhaps the most significant finding of the study. 'We found improvements between five and thirty-five IQ points, with an average improvement of 17.9 points ... we were convinced ... nutritional changes were the significant variable. They were making the children more intelligent and more emotionally stable.'

As the study above graphically illustrates, what you put into your body dramatically impacts the performance of your brain. So how can you ensure your body and brain are getting all the nutrients they need?

You need to eat a diet rich in foods that have specific value for the heart and cardiovascular system, the digestive system, the brain, and the nervous system. As you can begin to see from the vitamin Mind Map on the following page, the body needs to extract a wide range of nutrients from the food you eat for optimum performance.

Through the centuries – and despite the modern culture of faddy dieting – certain dietary principles have been discovered that are constant and common to all healthy eating and physical disciplines.

Eat fresh-picked food wherever possible. Fresh food has the advantage of being 'complete' and containing more vitamins, minerals, and nutrients than food that has been stored or tinned.

Eat a diet rich in variety. A varied diet allows your body to select from a wider range of possibilities those things it particularly needs at any moment in time. Eating the same foods regularly, or the same foods on certain given days, gives rise to the probability of over-providing the system with certain nutrients, or depleting some necessary element.

Look at yourself. On a regular basis stand naked, both front on and side on, in front of a mirror. Look at yourself objectively, and decide whether you look as healthy and fit as you should. If not, take appropriate dietary and other action; if you are satisfied with your appearance, continue the good practice!

'Listen' to yourself. Much of your eating behavior is simply habit. We often say 'yes' to every proffered snack or tit-bit, 'yes' to every possible cup of tea or coffee, and 'yes' to ourselves when looking at an item on the menu that we 'know we like'. When choosing food, especially in company, imagine that you are on your own, and go for food and drink which you would actually choose if you had the widest choice available and were eating what you really felt like.

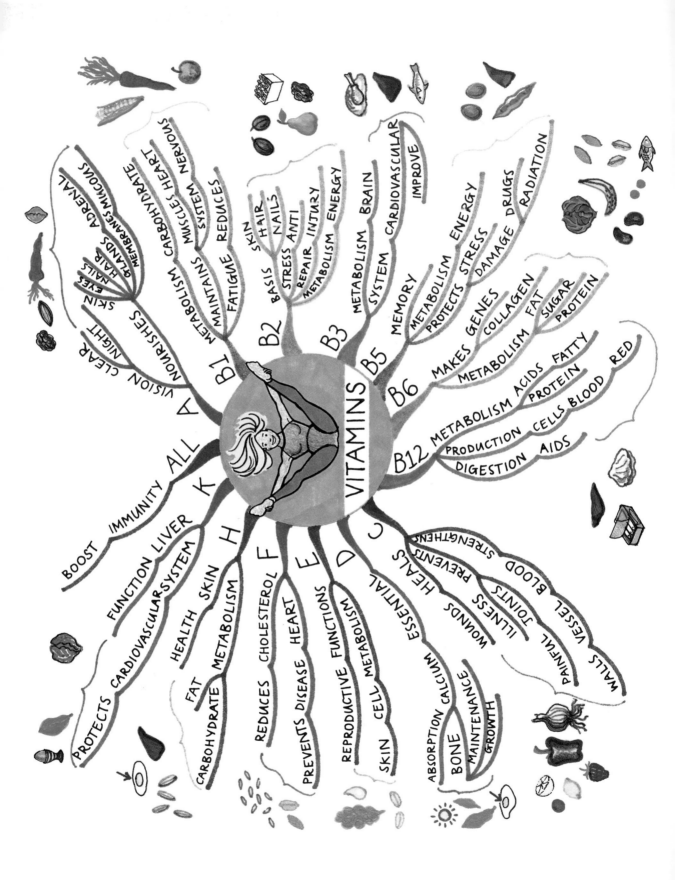

The following recommendations constitute a good basic diet for both your body and brain. Variations on these themes are an entirely personal matter, and should be explored with consideration and care for the ultimate benefit of your body.

## VEGETABLES AND FRUIT

Vegetables should form the base of any healthy diet. They are rich in nutrients, and contain ample fibre for cleansing the digestive tract and keeping it muscularly fit and flexible. They are quickly and easily digested, and can, if eaten sensibly, form a complete diet in themselves. Similarly, fruit should be included in a balanced diet.

## NUTS, SEEDS, AND WHOLE GRAINS

These are all highly concentrated sources of 'brain food'. Incidentally, since they contain all the genetic information necessary for plant life, they may in a sense be considered to be the brains of plants.

## FISH

Fish has traditionally been considered the 'brain food', and research by Professor Michael Crawford, Director of the Institute for Brain Chemistry and Human Nutrition, has confirmed this assumption. Around 60 percent of the brain is built from specialized fats (the lipids) or liquids, most of which we cannot manufacture in our own systems but have to take in from the food chain. The primary source of these essential fats is fish. Crawford goes so far as to posit the theory that the development of human intelligence and genius is largely due to the development of societies around lakes, river-basins, and coastlines, where there was an abundant supply of this essential brain food.

## MEAT

Meat can be highly nutritious, and should be eaten by those who choose to two or three times a week maximum. The danger with many meats is that they can be suffused with synthetic chemicals, and so it is better to eat organic meat, or wild meat and game where possible.

## BRAIN FOODS

Most of the foods mentioned in the basic healthy diet contain various items that are good for the brain (and what is good for your brain is good for your body!) Specifically, the brain and its nervous system are nourished by certain amino acids (the constituents of protein), the B complex of vitamins, the essential fats found abundantly in fish, and the minerals potassium, magnesium, iron, and zinc. Any healthy diet should include food that contains these essential nutrients.

The more aerobically fit your body is, the more your digestive system is able to ingest its food, and the more efficiently and effectively your blood can deliver the nutrients to your entire body and brain.

## THE INTELLIGENT DIET

The intelligent diet will naturally contain appropriate sugars and salts. It is therefore unnecessary and in many cases harmful to add additional salts and sugars to food; your body just doesn't need them. Similarly, any refined or processed food will tend to be more difficult to digest, and may contain elements that are damaging to your general health. It is also useful to restrict your intake of dairy and wheat products, neither of which the adult human digestive system is designed to cope with.

In addition to exercise and diet there is a third physical key when it comes to boosting your mental performance and that is the quality of rest that you allow your brain.

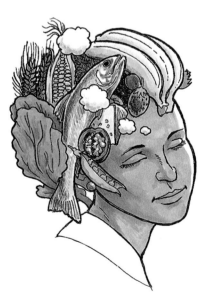

# Rest, Sleep, and Your Brain

Do you find that you tend to come up with your best ideas when you are:

→  In the bath?

→  Taking a shower?

→  Shaving?

→  Putting on make-up?

→  In bed?

→  Sleeping/dreaming?

→  Walking in the countryside?

→  Driving?

→  Jogging/swimming?

→  Doodling?

→  Listening to music?

**You are not alone!** Most people identify with at least one of the above, and the majority of people with most of them. This is because rest is a necessary part of mental as well as bodily function. Think of it as a mental breathing in and breathing out, where breathing in is equivalent to active learning and the assimilation of data, and breathing out is equivalent to sorting and integrating the information.

When you rest, your brain roams its internal Mind Maps, looking for and finding new associations to make new Mind Maps of thought.

This is why we are most creative and most capable of reviewing memories during rest, relaxation, and solitude. It is at these times that we can daydream about apples and gravity, bodies and water, sunbeams and the structure of the universe, and whatever great idea you next allow yourself to have.

In other words, to function most effectively, your brain needs regular breaks as well as regular periods of activity. If you do not take them, your brain will make you do so anyway – you might call it a loss of concentration, nervous tension, or (in more extreme cases) a nervous breakdown, but they are all instances of your brain insisting that you take a break and balance yourself.

Sleep, one of the deepest forms of rest, is a period where your brain integrates the day's experiences, shifting, sorting and filing, as well as solving problems. Dreams are a natural part of this process, and are one of the creative geniuses' greatest sources of inspiration.

**In a well-exercised and well-fed body, sleep will be deep and curative, and will often provide, from an infinite source of creativity, major insights and revelations.**

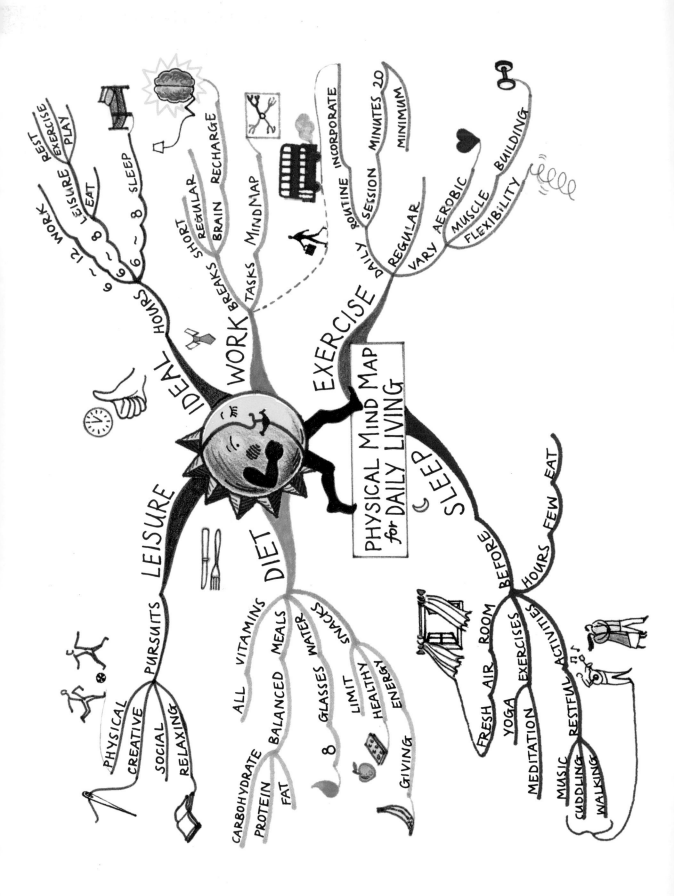

PHYSICAL MIND MAP for DAILY LIVING

**IDEAL**
HOURS
- WORK 9 ~ 12
- LEISURE 8 ~ 9
- EAT 8
- SLEEP 6 ~ 8
- REST
- EXERCISE
- PLAY

**WORK**
- BREAKS SHORT
- REGULAR
- BRAIN RECHARGE
- TASKS MINDMAP

**EXERCISE**
- DAILY ROUTINE INCORPORATE
- SESSION MINUTES 20 MINIMUM
- REGULAR
- VARY AEROBIC
- MUSCLE BUILDING
- FLEXIBILITY

**SLEEP**
- BEFORE
  - ROOM FRESH AIR
  - EXERCISES YOGA
  - MEDITATION
- HOURS FEW EAT
- RESTFUL ACTIVITIES
  - MUSIC
  - CUDDLING
  - WALKING

**DIET**
- ALL VITAMINS
- MEALS BALANCED
  - CARBOHYDRATE
  - PROTEIN
  - FAT
- WATER 8 GLASSES
- SNACKS
  - LIMIT
  - HEALTHY ENERGY GIVING

**LEISURE**
- PURSUITS
  - PHYSICAL
  - CREATIVE
  - SOCIAL
  - RELAXING

# Mind Map Motivator

 **It is one thing knowing that you need to care for your body to nurture the performance of your mind, and quite another putting a health plan into action.**

How can you plan your physical regime and motivate yourself to stick to it? With a Mind Map of course! A Mind Map will always strengthen and clarify the Mind Maps of thought in your head.

The Mind Map exercises below are specific to motivating yourself to make health and lifestyle changes, but you could of course use Mind Maps to motivate yourself to achieve anything you want.

Before you start the motivational Mind Map exercise, study the Mind Map on the following page. It offers a brief overview of the kind of balance you should be looking to achieve to fine-tune your mental performance.

MIND MAP OF MOTIVATION

STARS — INTELLIGENCE — PHYSICAL — SCHUMACHER / JAGGER / FIENNES

LIFE — CHALLENGES — MEET / AMBITIONS — FULFIL / MAXIMUM GAIN

HEALTH — INCREASED LIFE — QUALITY / EXPECTANCY
HEALTH — IMMUNITY — IMPROVED SYSTEMS — STRENGTH / STAMINA / POISE / FLEXIBILITY / SLEEP / SENSES

ENERGY — GREATER — MENTAL / PHYSICAL

EMOTIONS — BALANCED — POSITIVE / CONTROLLED STRESS

APPEARANCE — FIT / ATTRACTIVE / RADIANT

BENEFITS — INTELLIGENCE — SPATIAL / SENSUAL / CREATIVE / PERSONAL / SOCIAL

# Mind Map Exercise: Motivate Yourself to Change

In Chapter Four you learned about thinking positively to help your brain succeed and the same goes for motivating yourself to improve aspects of your diet, exercise, and sleep routines.

If you need to make changes to how you look after your body, start by drawing a Mind Map of all the positive reasons why you want to nurture yourself physically.

Start by drawing a central image to focus your Mind Map – you might choose yourself or simply a positive symbol. Add branches to your Mind Map to explore all the different positive reasons to change. How will it improve your overall health? Make a note of all the benefits you will enjoy both mentally and physically. Do you think you will feel more confident if you are fitter? Are there any role models in your life to whom you can aspire – people you know or public personalities whom you admire? What do you think you can achieve when you have more energy and better mental alertness? Could you get a promotion? Would you take a course in night school? Keep brainstorming positive reasons for change until your Mind Map is overflowing with ideas.

When you are satisfied with your Mind Map pin it up somewhere prominent where you will be able to look at it every day – or scan it into your computer and set it as your desktop at work. Keep referring back to it to keep all the positive reasons for change fresh in your mind.

When you refer back to your Mind Map you'll be feeding your increasingly growing Mind Maps of thought about why you are motivated to change.

# Mind Map Exercise: Put Together a Plan of Action

When you have drawn your motivational Mind Map you can draw a Mind Map to work out your action plan.

Start by drawing a central image of yourself as you imagine you will be when you make the changes to your diet, fitness, and relaxation habits. Next draw branches to represent the main aspects of your plan that you are going to start, for example 'diet', 'rest', or 'exercise'.

Next explore these with sub-branches to work out how you are going to fit these around your current routine. For example, what will your new exercise routine involve? The gym? Swimming? Cycling? How often will you do it? Will you train on set days? Will you do it on your own at home, as part of an exercise class, or do you have a friend who will be training with you? What sort of small lifestyle changes can you make? Could you take the stairs to your work or flat instead of the lift? Can you walk to the shops rather than drive? Keep exploring your branches and developing your plan to get fit until you are satisfied it will work. Then pick a day and start – keeping your Mind Maps handy to stack on track and monitor your progress.

As you have seen over the last five chapters, Mind Maps are the power tool when it comes to unlocking your full potential. The next chapter shows you just some of the ways that Mind Maps in action can help you deliver your best.

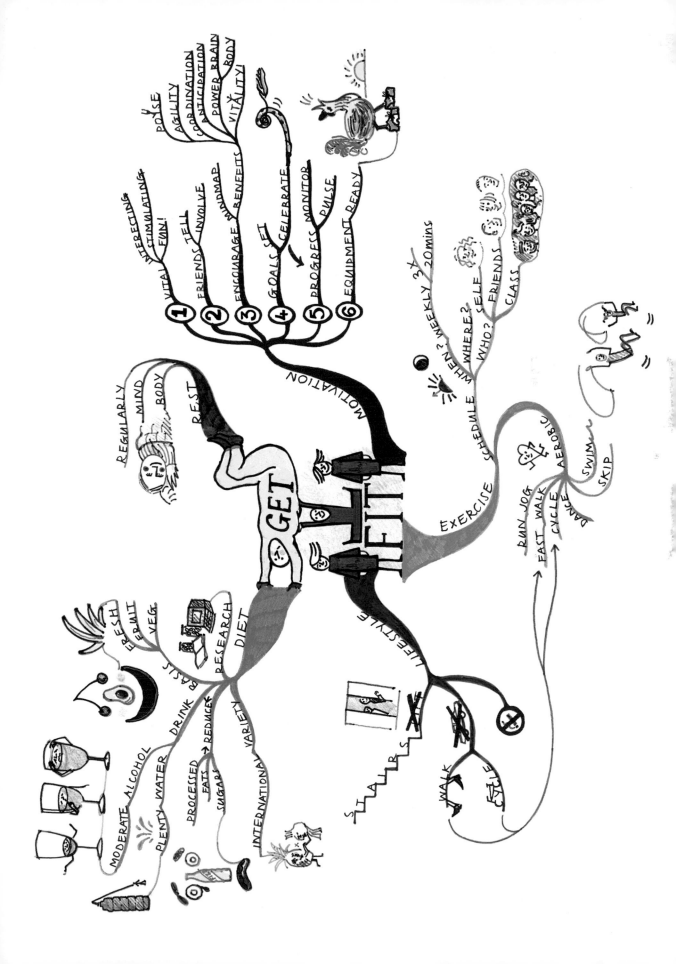

# Mind Maps for Everyday Success

# Overview of Chapter 6:

Mind Maps for Work

Mind Maps for Your Social Life

Mind Maps for Life

You are now more than ready to explore the exciting world of Mind Map applications and how they can add quality, effectiveness, and success to your personal, family, professional, and daily life.

Over the previous chapters you have discovered the science behind Mind Maps – how they tap into your brain's own preferred methods of learning, associating, imagining, creating, and remembering. Mind Maps are the brain's perfect cognitive tool.

Mind Maps bring you many advantages. They save you time, allow you to organize and clarify your thinking, generate new ideas, keep track of things, dramatically improve your memory and concentration, stimulate more of your brain, and allow you to keep your eye on the 'whole picture'. And, most importantly, they are fun to do!

In this chapter I am going to show you how you can put all these advantages to work for you every day.

You will learn some of the ways in which you can apply this master-thinking technique to a whole range of the most important life skills including planning, studying, problem-solving, coming to new realizations and awareness, and even dreaming.

This chapter gives you ideas of how you can use Mind Maps in everyday work situations, such as in meetings and during networking opportunities, and will help you to make the best, most productive use of your time.

**Mind Maps aren't just work tools – they can help you plan and organize your social and personal life too, not to mention helping your creativity to soar to amazing new heights. Here you will find hints on how to use Mind Maps to learn a new language, design a garden, and even to visualize your own life plan.**

This chapter is designed to be as practical and useful as Mind Maps are themselves. You will find examples of how to Mind Map a dozen or so common situations, for you to consult and dip in and out of as needed. Each example is illustrated to help spark your imagination and enable you to create your own unique Mind Map. Remember that there is no one correct answer when it comes to the content of your Mind Maps – there are only specific guidelines on how you should draw them as outlined in Chapter One. Make sure that you follow these guidelines as closely as possible as they are there to help your brain radiate its fantastic ideas.

Not every conceivable occasion where Mind Maps are valuable is covered here, of course – that would require a book of infinite size, limited only by your own limitless imagination, which you know is limitless! However, you will find that the principles behind Mind Mapping are easily applied to each and every unique situation.

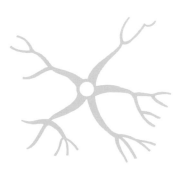

# Mind Maps for Work

 **Mind Maps are ideal work tools. They enable you to plan, organize, schedule, and brainstorm more memorably and efficiently than ever before. Every business should use them!**

Here are just a few examples of how Mind Maps can boost your performance at work, helping you to ever-greater success.

## RUNNING A MEETING

Planning and running a meeting, regardless of whether it's a business meeting for a few colleagues, a social club annual general meeting, or a full-blown conference complete with outside speakers and delegates, can be a stressful business. There are so many things to schedule and organize and keep track of that it's very easy to forget some small but crucial detail amidst all the kerfuffle and excitement.

In these sorts of situations, Mind Maps are ideal. They can be used to plan all the different stages involved in organizing the meeting, so that you can be sure that everything is done in the right order and on time – vital if participants are attending from several different countries and their travel arrangements have to be coordinated across time zones!

Take a large sheet of paper, and in the center draw an image that best represents your meeting – a flipchart, whiteboard, graph, or whatever. Then radiate main branches off the image detailing the main areas you have to organize: the names of those attending, where the meeting is to be held, the time and date of the

meeting, supplies and equipment that will be needed (coffee, water, paper, lunch, AV equipment, etc.), the subject and agenda of the meeting, and so on.

Off each main branch you can then radiate sub-branches detailing decisions made (Room X; 2.30 p.m. on Tuesday 17th). It can also be useful to add in time limits for the branch topics, especially if the meeting is to be big or complex to organize, so that you can see at a glance when each stage has to be completed by – the location has to be booked by X date; the attendees have to be informed by Y and have to confirm their attendance by Z so that appropriate transport and accommodation can be firmly booked and the agenda and briefing papers can be circulated in time to be read, for example.

When you're attending a meeting Mind Maps can be used as a method of taking effective, memorable notes. Use different colour pens and put one-word points into circles, triangles, dodecahedrons – any shapes that appeal to you – rather than taking normal, boring, monochrome, instantly forgettable linear notes. Your later recall will be vastly improved, and your concentration at the meeting itself will be sharper. Your brain will be awake and alert!

Mind Maps make excellent speaking plans, too, if you have to give any sort of presentation (something many, many people dread). Mapping your thoughts out beforehand using a Mind Map will ensure that you are fully on top of your brief: your mind will naturally make connections between your points using a Mind Map, and so you will find it easy to remember them, which will boost your confidence in your own speech.

# JOB INTERVIEW

Preparing for and attending a job interview is often high up on many people's lists of things they least like doing – especially if you really want or need this particular job!

However, there are a lot of things you can do to boost your confidence and your chances of being offered the job, and drawing a Mind Map to help you prepare is one of them.

Mind Maps are especially good tools to use to think around possible questions you might be asked in the interview. Because you've Mind Mapped your thoughts already, you'll have answers in your head, which, thanks to the Mind Map's synchronicity with your brain's way of thinking and remembering, you'll be able to confidently give, even if the specific question is not one you'd thought of before. Your brain will be primed to associate ideas and link themes together.

No one can predict precisely each and every question asked in a job interview, but four of the most common ones are as follows:

➡ Why are you applying for this job?

➡ What can you do for the company?

➡ What kind of person are you?

➡ Why do you think you are the right person for this position?

There are five additional questions which are often asked too:

➡ Where would you like to be in five years' time?

➡ What are your strengths and weaknesses?

➡ How would you describe yourself?

→ Why did you leave your last job/do you want to leave your present job?

→ What do you know about the company?

Take a few of these questions and Mind Map out your answers to see just how much Mind Maps can help you prepare.

For example, take the question 'Why do you think you are the right person for this position?' Draw an image to represent the job in the centre of a large sheet of paper – remember to make it relevant, so if you're applying for a job as a clothes-store manager, you could draw an image of a suit. Then, on curving branches radiating out from the central image, note down all the key requirements, the job description lists, together with any other key qualities you think a manager should have. Next, radiate from each branch, sub-branches noting all your strengths, qualifications, and previous work experience that show you meet (exceed!) each of the job's requirements.

'What do you know about the company' or 'What can you do for the company' are questions where you can shine in an interview – provided you've done your research. Mind Maps are perfect for organizing this research into a useful, useable, memorable form – especially if you're applying to and researching several companies at once (often the situation if you are about to graduate).

Draw the company's logo, or a relevant image representing the company in the centre of a large sheet of paper, and radiate out main branches covering such subjects as products, markets, suppliers, sales, profits, ethos, and image. Then add in the fruits of your research on the sub-branches to build up a comprehensive picture of the organization.

You can go into any interview confident and well prepared, using such Mind Maps!

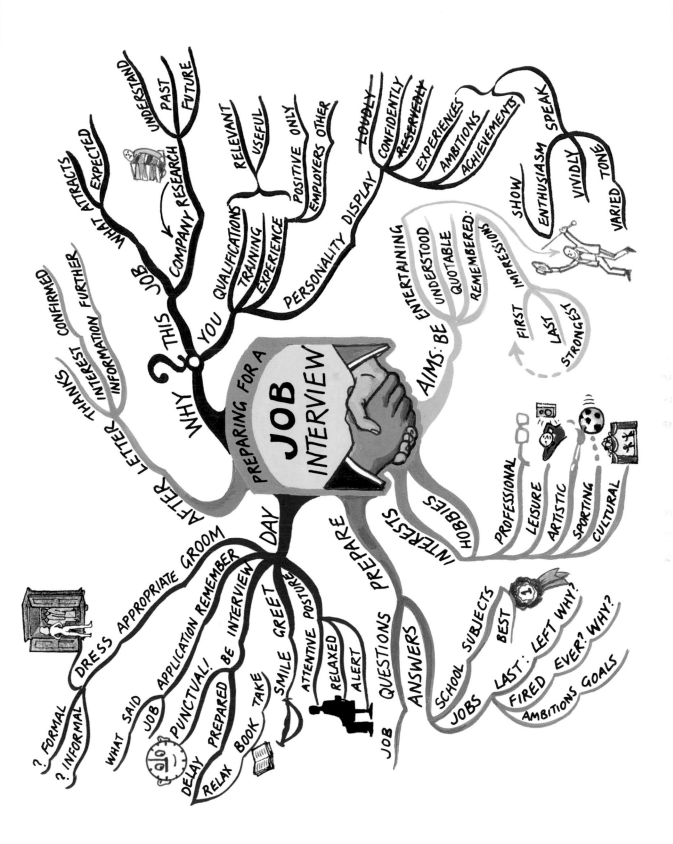

PREPARING FOR A **JOB INTERVIEW**

WHY? THIS JOB
- UNDERSTAND — PAST, FUTURE
- WHAT EXPECTED
- WHAT ATTRACTS
- COMPANY RESEARCH

YOU
- QUALIFICATIONS — RELEVANT, USEFUL
- TRAINING
- EXPERIENCE — POSITIVE ONLY, EMPLOYERS OTHER
- PERSONALITY DISPLAY

AFTER LETTER
- THANKS CONFIRMED
- INTEREST FURTHER
- INFORMATION

DISPLAY
- LOUDLY
- CONFIDENTLY
- RESERVEDLY
- EXPERIENCES
- AMBITIONS
- ACHIEVEMENTS

SPEAK
- SHOW ENTHUSIASM
- VIVIDLY
- VARIED TONE

AIMS: BE
- ENTERTAINING
- UNDERSTOOD
- QUOTABLE
- REMEMBERED:
- FIRST IMPRESSIONS
- LAST STRONGEST

HOBBIES / INTERESTS
- PROFESSIONAL
- LEISURE
- ARTISTIC
- SPORTING
- CULTURAL

DAY
- DRESS APPROPRIATE GROOM — ? FORMAL, ? INFORMAL
- REMEMBER — WHAT SAID, JOB APPLICATION
- BE INTERVIEW — PUNCTUAL!, DELAY, PREPARED, RELAX, TAKE BOOK
- GREET — SMILE
- ATTENTIVE POSTURE — RELAXED, ALERT

PREPARE
- QUESTIONS
- ANSWERS
- JOB — SCHOOL SUBJECTS BEST
- JOBS LAST: LEFT WHY?
- FIRED EVER? WHY?
- AMBITIONS GOALS

# WRITING AN ESSAY

Mind Maps are an excellent tool for helping you write well-structured and focussed essays. They are particularly helpful as they enable you to see the whole picture of your argument and objectively assess if your argument and the structure of your essay are logical. Not only can Mind Maps help you to plan what you intend to write, but they are also a useful tool when it comes to writing your essay out in full: you can keep referring back to it to check you are on track.

Start by drawing a central image that embodies the content of what you need to write. Think about all the research you have done and the information you have gathered from it and allow your brain to daydream about it. If you like, you can add an 'information' branch to your Mind Map and write down the main strands of information that you have gathered.

Next draw branches on your Mind Map to represent your introduction, central argument, and conclusion. Look at the themes you have jotted down on your 'information' branch and think about how it could all hang together. Unless you prefer to work out your introduction first, explore your 'central argument' branch with sub-branches to help you build the main body of information in your text. Once you have established the meat of your argument you can go back and work out your introduction and conclusion.

Keep taking a mental step back from your Mind Map to check that the argument or themes of your essay are progressing in a coherent way. Once you are satisfied with your Mind Map you can begin writing it, keeping your Mind Map beside you to stay on track.

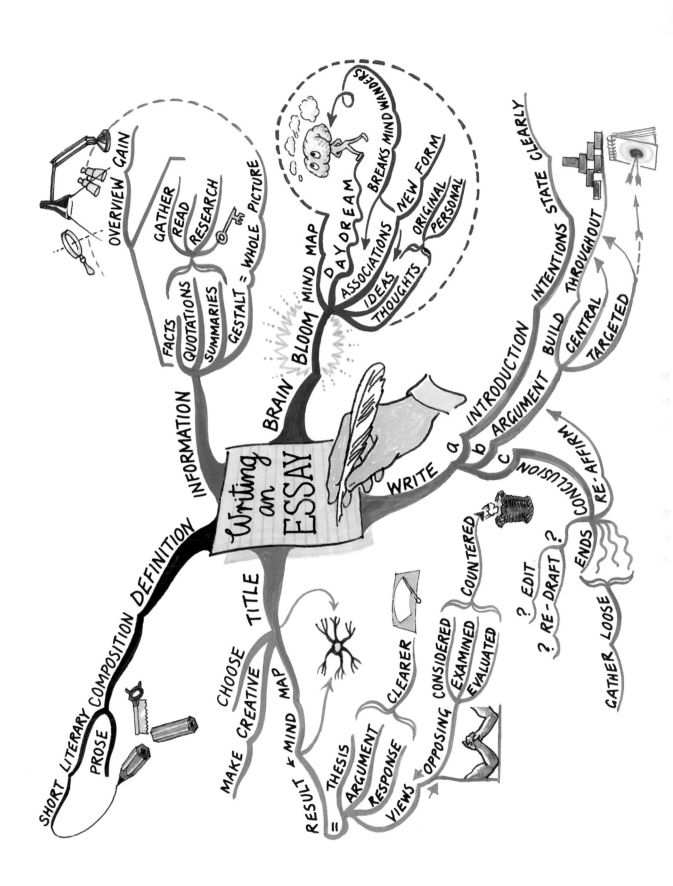

# Mind Maps in Action

## MIND MAPS IN THE CLASSROOM

Ruth is a Spanish teacher from York. She uses Mind Maps in the classroom to help her pupils learn role-plays for different situations:

*'I have always found Mind Maps very helpful in the classroom. They are fantastic for summarizing information on a single page in a fun and accessible way, and the simple act of drawing one seems to make it easier for them to memorize information.*

*I find them particularly helpful when it comes to role-play scenarios as my pupils can have the key vocabulary on the page in front of them, but not get fixated on reading phrases from their books word for word.*

*When it comes to exam time, we always Mind Map each situation and explore the different possibilities that might come up for scenarios, adding all the necessary vocabulary. My pupils are always more confident and competent when it comes to their oral examinations.'*

# Mind Maps in Action

## MIND MAPS MAKE POWERFUL BUSINESS PLANS

Dwain Dunnell is the man behind the weight-loss system, Slimtone. He always uses Mind Maps to create his successful business plans:

*'All my business plans in the past were lists. It's very difficult because the brain doesn't work like a list. If you make a Mind Map for the week or a Mind Map for the day, you can see the route that you need to take to achieve your objective.*

*Using Mind Maps, I did my entire business plan all the way up to £20 million in a year's time, in half an hour. Mind Maps are powerful because they enable us to influence. Influence gives us power and power allows us to achieve our goals.*

*If you can learn how a Mind Map works then you'll learn how your own brain works.'*

# STARTING A NEW VENTURE

Mind Maps are fantastic planning tools. They enable you to see the 'whole picture' and ensure that nothing is left to chance. What better way, then, to plan a new venture?

Perhaps you are thinking of starting up your own business, like a store or a company. Or perhaps you want to do something on a smaller scale, like starting up a babysitting service or a kids after-school club. Whatever your idea, Mind Maps can help you plan smarter and be more successful.

There are so many things to consider when you are starting up a new venture. It can be a really daunting task. However, if you use a Mind Map you can make sure you have thought everything through carefully first. For example, where will you locate your business? Do you need your own premises or can you work from home? And what about staff? Do you need to employ other people or can you manage alone? How will you finance your venture? Will it take a lot of start-up capital? Do you need to borrow money? All of these issues can be plotted out on your Mind Map, using the key words for each of the main things you have to consider. This will allow you to see problems before they arise, and take the necessary steps to avoid them.

As your venture develops, you can use your Mind Map with the TEFCAS success model as a constant point of reference to check that things stay on track. For example, very often your finances and cash flow take up so much time and importance that it is easy to forget all the brilliant ideas you had for making money in the first place. You may leave all the marketing ideas you had to one side (ironically, it is these very marketing initiatives that could increase your revenue). But if you refer to your Mind Map on a regular basis, you will not forget any of your initial ideas, and you will be able to implement them when the time is right.

**With a Mind Map at your side, you are giving your new venture a head start to success.**

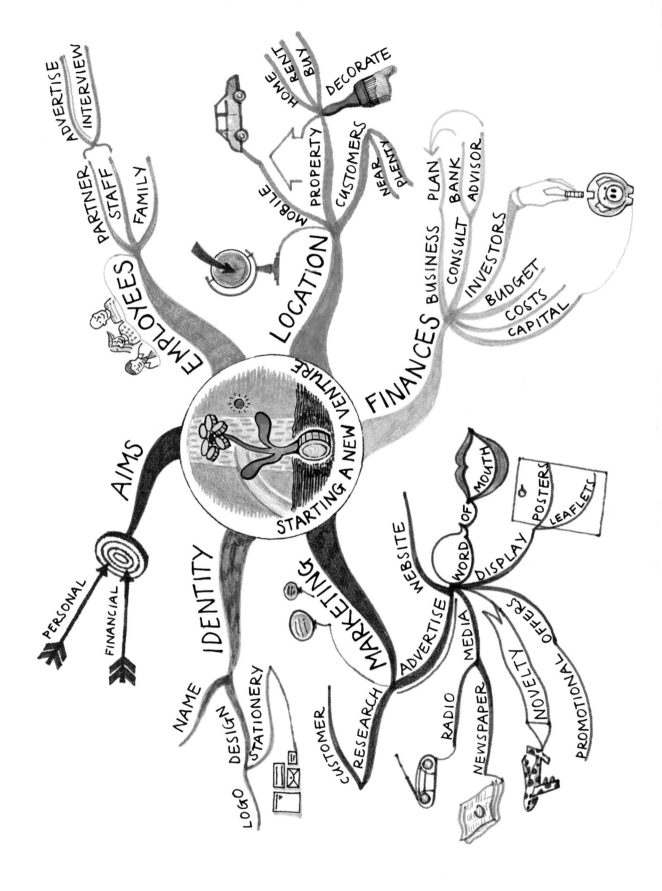

STARTING A NEW VENTURE

EMPLOYEES
ADVERTISE
INTERVIEW
PARTNER
STAFF
FAMILY

LOCATION
HOME
RENT
BUY
DECORATE
MOBILE
PROPERTY
CUSTOMERS
NEAR
PLENTY

FINANCES
BUSINESS PLAN
CONSULT BANK
ADVISOR
INVESTORS
BUDGET
COSTS
CAPITAL

AIMS
PERSONAL
FINANCIAL

IDENTITY
NAME
LOGO
DESIGN
STATIONERY

MARKETING
CUSTOMER
RESEARCH
ADVERTISE
WEBSITE
WORD OF MOUTH
DISPLAY
POSTERS
LEAFLETS
MEDIA
RADIO
NEWSPAPER
NOVELTY
PROMOTIONAL OFFERS

# NETWORKING

The art of networking is crucial in today's business world. Contacts made and nurtured in all walks of life and in all sorts of situations can set you up for work success and career advancement months or even years hence. And, of course, networking can expand and enrich your social circle too.

Unfortunately, many people dread the very idea of business 'networking'. However, with some planning and preparation (and we already know how useful Mind Maps are for this), and some careful 'follow-up', networking can be not only very productive but also enjoyable.

Networking is all about self-presentation. What sort of image do you want to present? Confident? Yes. Efficient? Yes. Memorable? Certainly. How can you project your 'self-image' to other people? First impressions count an awful lot: your clothes and your body language can say so much about you. In the same way, last impressions are also very important – you want to leave people with good, positive, memorable memories of meeting you. Mind Map your ideal self-image and how you can present it to others, and see what strategies you come up with and can brainstorm.

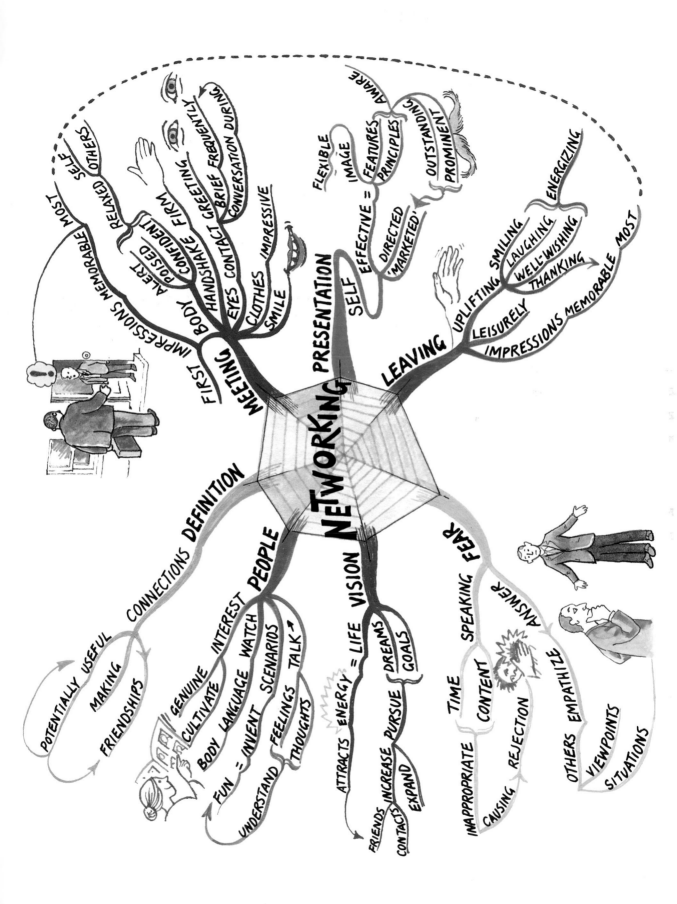

How do you remember all the people you meet, their names, details, how you met them, their interests, hobbies, and line of work? Easy! With Mind Maps!

If you go to a party or conference and meet many useful contacts among the other guests, Mind Map it afterwards. Start with a memorable central image to sum up the event. Radiate off the image curving main branches, each one with the name of a new contact. Then you can carry on adding sub-branches detailing each person's interests, work, physical features, and so on.

In this way, you'll be able to 'place' each person instantly when you meet them again, and they'll be very impressed by your knowledge and memory.

You can use this technique before an event as well, to research the backgrounds of people whom you know are going to be attending – 'forewarned is forearmed'. If you use Mind Maps to do your homework on the other guests, you put yourself at an advantage with your knowledge, and so can relax and shine amidst the company!

# Mind Maps for Your Social Life

Organizing a busy social life is an enormous task in itself, and Mind Maps can take the stress out of the planning – just as they do in your work life.

# SHOPPING FOR GIFTS

The holiday season is full of fun and magic, but sometimes it can be tricky to buy everybody what they want. How often have you gone out shopping for your family and come back with something far more suitable for you than them? A Mind Map is the perfect tool to work out what to buy your family and friends, and you can tick off each person as you find each gift – there will be no danger of forgetting anybody!

Start by drawing a central image that symbolizes gifts or giving. Next add main branches of the people that you need to shop for. Explore each person in turn with sub-branches. Do they have any hobbies? If so, what sort of gifts or gadgets can you think of that relate to that hobby? What do you know they like or dislike? What did you buy them last holiday season? Was that popular? Could you get them something that builds on that present? Have they made any suggestions? Have you heard them wishing for things earlier in the year? Add a branch to sum up possible options. Once you have brainstormed that person, start on the next, and so on until you have Mind Mapped everybody you need.

With your Mind Map you should be able to come up with excellent gift ideas for all the family – but remember to keep it hidden from eager eyes! Take your Mind Map with you when you go shopping and tick off each person as you find their presents.

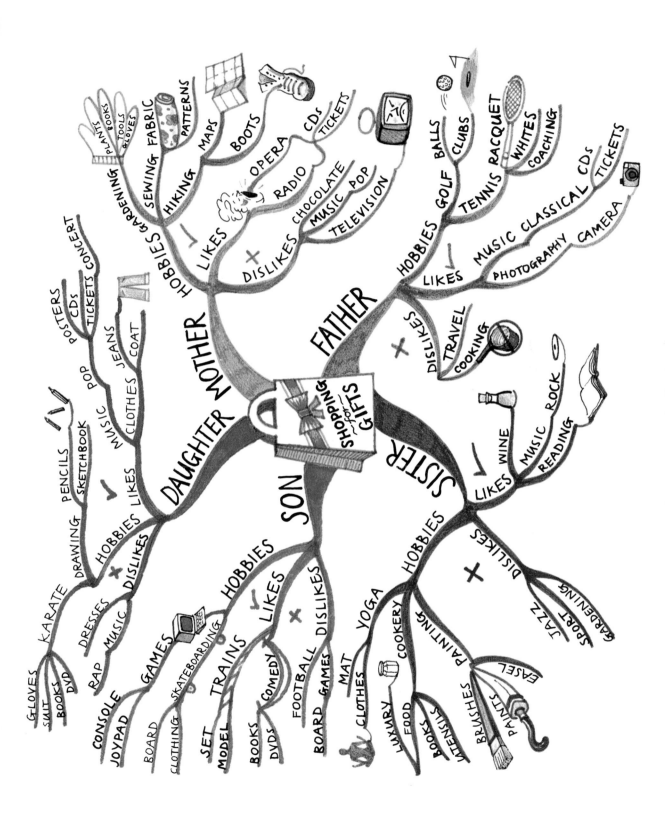

# A ROMANTIC WEEKEND

Planning a romantic weekend can cause a lot of anxiety and stress, because it is so important that such events are wonderfully successful. As with any other form of planning, if any vital ingredient is missing or forgotten, the whole event could be a catastrophe. This is where Mind Maps can come to the rescue!

With your Romantic Weekend Mind Map radiate, from a suitably romantic central image, the main branches of the things you need to consider.

These will include location, travel, activities, food, drinks, equipment (including clothes, toiletries, books, and games), and special surprises, etc.

Perhaps the main advantage of the Mind Map for planning the romantic weekend is that it gives a much greater probability that the weekend will be a success, and simultaneously gives you more confidence and less stress.

The confident and relaxed individual is a much more attractive romantic partner!

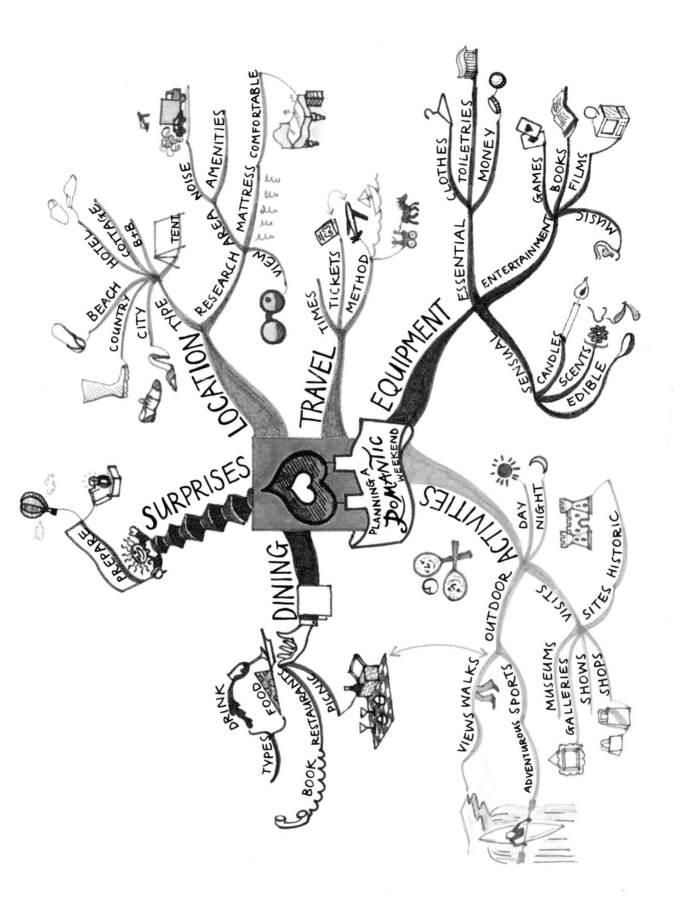

Planning a **Romantic** Weekend

LOCATION
- Type
  - Hotel
  - B+B
  - Cottage
  - Tent
  - Beach
  - Country
  - City
- Research Area
  - Noise
  - Amenities
  - Mattress
  - Comfortable
  - View

TRAVEL
- Times
- Tickets
- Method

EQUIPMENT
- Essential
  - Clothes
  - Toiletries
  - Money
- Entertainment
  - Games
  - Books
  - Films
  - Music
- Sensual
  - Candles
  - Scents
  - Edible

ACTIVITIES
- Day
- Night
- Outdoor
  - Views
  - Walks
  - Adventurous Sports
- Visits
  - Museums
  - Galleries
  - Shows
  - Shops
  - Sites Historic

DINING
- Types
- Drink
- Food
- Book Restaurant
- Picnic

SURPRISES
- Prepare

# Mind Maps in Action

## DESIGNING A DREAM NURSERY

Josh and Stephanie used Mind Maps to design a dream nursery for their unborn baby boy:

*'The room that we wanted to use as a nursery had been Josh's study for years and it was hard to see its potential as a nursery for our baby amidst all the stacks of papers and books.*

*One evening as we were chatting after dinner we decided to Mind Map how we would like to change the room and make it the perfect nursery. Our ideas were soon flowing freely, so much so that we had to tape a couple more sheets of paper together and add them to our original Mind Map!*

*Suddenly we could see the potential of Josh's pokey little office – and we even came up with solutions for what we could do with everything we'd move out of the office.*

*I can't say that we used every idea that we Mind Mapped – installing a nappy-chute to the outside rubbish bin would have been a little extreme! – but the Mind Map certainly helped us plan the best possible nursery for our little boy.'*

# Mind Maps in Action

## WORK–LIFE BALANCE

Rosalind Gower is a working mother who is a television producer at the BBC. She uses Mind Maps to keep her work and family life in balance:

*'Mind Maps have changed my whole life. As a working mother, you are always being torn in loads of different directions, so if I set up a home Mind Map with "work" branches and "kids" branches and all the other responsibilities that working mothers have, I don't forget anything. If you say to yourself, "I must book a dental appointment", you just stick it in the relevant branch of the Mind Map.*

*And at work, when I start any new project, I have a whole variety of information and so it's important to try and categorize that and get people working on different aspects. I use a Mind Map and that is really effective: everybody is responsible for one branch of the Mind Map and I am at the centre overseeing it all. It is very successful.'*

# LEARNING A FOREIGN LANGUAGE

More and more of us are living and holidaying abroad, or travelling either on business or for pleasure, and more and more of us are learning a foreign language such as Spanish or French.

Having very successfully learned one language at a very young age (your native tongue!), people often struggle to learn another one so easily when they get older. They've forgotten how readily, naturally, and hungrily their brains learn.

You, however, know exactly how your brain works. How it uses imagery and association. How repetition increases the probability of repetition, and how using both sides of your brain – the more logical left-hand side and the more creative right-hand side – create a tremendous synergetic effect on your brain power.

You also know that Mind Maps are the most brain-friendly tools with which you can work – when you Mind Map in a foreign language you are Mind Mapping the images, networks, and associations of *that* language directly into your mind.

Create colorful Mind Maps, full of imagery and association, around specific topics like shopping, travel, and eating out, to reinforce your ever-expanding vocabulary and understanding.

Draw a central image of the topic you wish to master – 'Travel' for example. Then radiate off the image main branches covering subjects such as going by train, plane, car, your destination, and directions. Next draw sub-branches of associated words from each main branch: for example, with the main branch 'train' sub-branches could cover 'station', 'platform', 'tickets', etc., each illustrated and labelled using your new vocabulary. Further sub-branches can be drawn to illustrate (for example) buying tickets, asking how much they cost, first or second class, and so forth.

In this way you will be able to build up complete phrases and sentences that you will recall, remember, and repeat effortlessly.

Learning a Language

LEARNING → LOVE = CURIOSITY INSATIABLE

?

PLAY
ENJOYABLE
IMAGINATIVE AMUSING ALWAYS
WORDS
DIFFERENT SECTIONS
MIX
= NEW COMBINATIONS
NEW

BRAIN PRINCIPLE
MIMICKING
VOCABULARY RATE INCREASES
ASSOCIATIONS NEW MADE
MIMICKING

PROGRESSIVE SCHEMES
STRUCTURED GRAMMAR IMAGINATIVE
MINDMAP

IMMERSION
TRAVEL
LIVE
ABROAD

MISTAKES
ENJOY = LEARNING
PERSIST
OVERCOME OBSTACLES = LEARNING

# YOUR DAUGHTER'S WEDDING

As any parents who have organized their daughter's wedding know, the Big Day takes an awful lot of careful preparation – and the more traditional the ceremony, the more elaborate the preparations, which start months, if not a full year, before!

There is just so much to remember to do.

The ceremony has to be decided upon – traditional church wedding or registry office? – the date, how many bridesmaids or attendants, what sort of music to play, how many guests can fit in if it is a small space? The reception venue has to be booked (often before the ceremony itself!) and all the catering arranged. The Dress has to be chosen and ordered, and the groom's, bridesmaids', and ushers' outfits decided upon.

There are flowers to arrange, and cars to hire, and guest lists to make and invitations to send out, and photographs to order, and ... and ... and ...

Luckily, drawing a Master Mind Map of the great event can reduce the workload and the stress levels immensely. Start with a resonant central image and radiate branches out for each of the main aspects of the wedding – the ceremony, the reception, the dress, flowers, guests, invitations, and so on. Subsequent sub-branches can be made detailing what has been decided and what needs to be done, and when.

Drawing such a Mind Map will help the day go off smoothly and easily, and will allow you all to relax and enjoy the happy occasion.

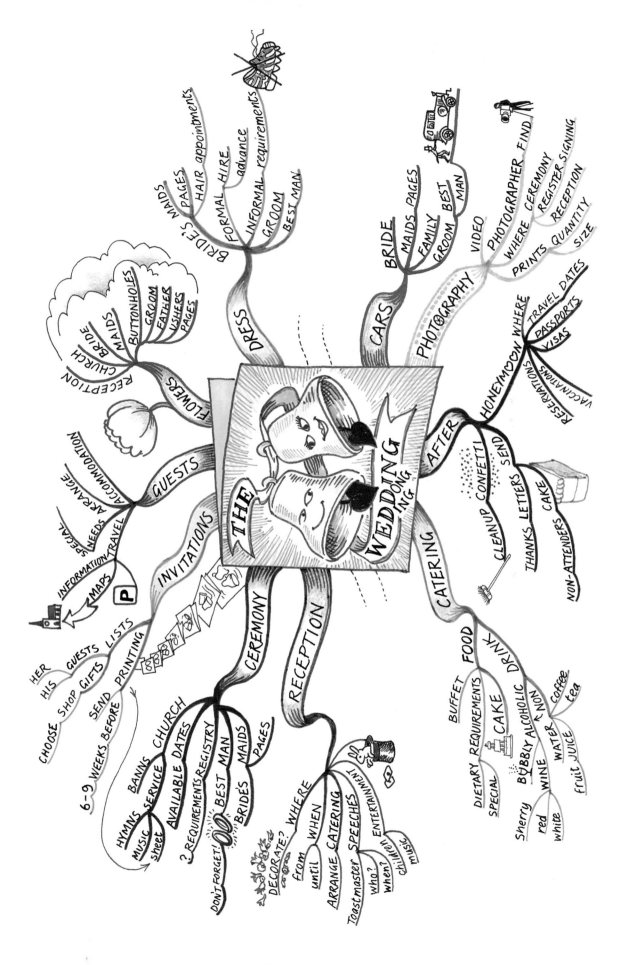

# DESIGNING YOUR GARDEN

Mind Maps are not just useful for organizing and planning – they are wonderful creative stimulants!

Designing a garden is a wonderful opportunity to let your imagination run riot, and drawing a Mind Map of your ideas will allow all sorts of weird and wonderful associations to germinate and grow.

Start with a central image that represents your ideal garden, and see where your imagination takes you. Map out its shape, areas (flower borders, vegetable patch, fruit trees, compost heap, storage and working corners), features (a pond? a seating area? a pergola covered with roses? an arboretum?), what sort of plants you would like flowering at what times of year, whether you want a low-maintenance garden you can sit and entertain in, or whether you would like one you could potter about in, tending your plants. The sky is your limit!

And once you have dreamed up your ideal, you can then draw a Mind Map to plan it into reality. Where can you get your plants from? Are they exotic specimens that will require particular soil conditions? Which plants need planting when to ensure all-round colour and interest in your garden? All these considerations can be formulated, decided upon, and organized with the aid of a Mind Map. Moreover, you'll have a handy aide-mémoire when you go plant hunting!

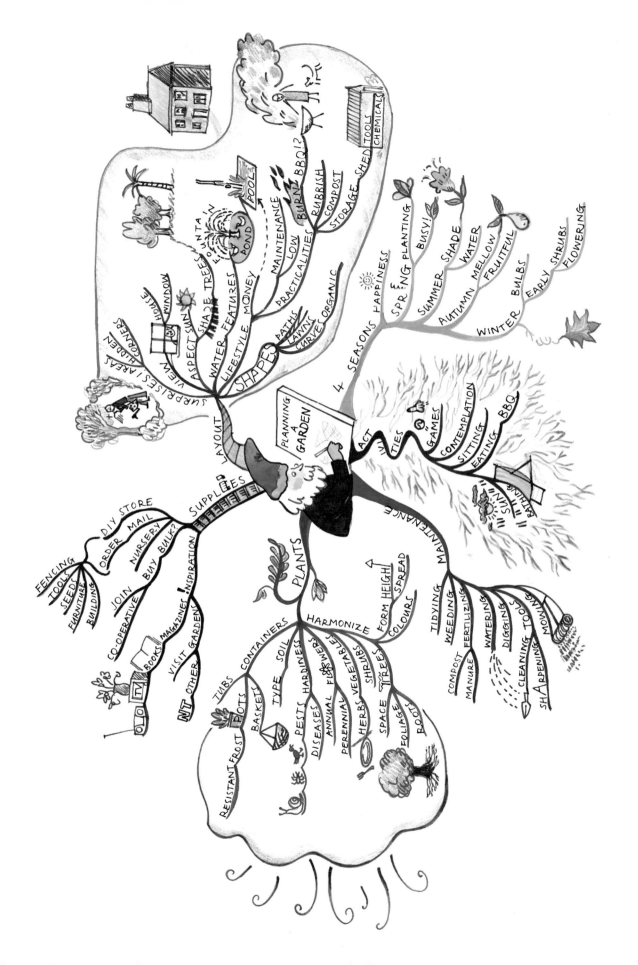

# Mind Maps for Life

## PLANNING FAMILY EVENTS

A dear friend of mine uses Mind Maps to plan all her family's daily, weekly, annual, and special events.

Her Mind Maps appear in a place, commonly known as the community hub of the family and where they are increasingly to be found: on her fridge door!

She, in her own words, will tell you how she uses them, what for, and what the advantages are.

'Before I had heard about Tony and his Mind Maps, I was in chaos! I consider myself a pretty typical twenty-first century woman – I want it all! I am a wife, a mother, I have a career, I like to keep fit and I love my social life. Everything has equal importance and I enjoy all the demands and successes. And I certainly don't want to miss out on anything, least of all any of my son's important activities – be they studying for exams, attending a concert, helping him with his art project, or making sure his hair is cut in time for the school photo!

However, I realized that wanting it all meant that I had to be super-efficient in my organization at home. While packing my briefcase for the following day's meetings, had I remembered to *pick up the dry-cleaned suit for my husband's important meeting the next day, or that the dog's appointment with the vet was at 3.00 p.m. at precisely the same time as I had an important meeting, so who was going to take him? And which day of the week was it in my son's school schedule? If tomorrow was Wednesday, he needed his football boots and his piano music and would need to be picked up later than usual as he was in the school musical rehearsal and then when he came home he had homework to do before supper, bath and bed! Oh, and my mother was arriving for two days – must make sure the guest bed had clean sheets on and get in more food, and send off the deposit for our vacation or we would lose the reservation! And remember to call Susie to tell her that I can't join her at the yoga class after all because of all of the above.*

*Most of the time, we somehow muddled through (with frantic phone calls from the school about some vital piece of equipment that had been forgotten and equally frantic calls from my husband reminding me of that important business dinner that, yes, I had forgotten about). Then I heard about Mind Maps. I couldn't think what on earth these could possibly be, but was sold on the idea that on one piece of paper I could map out our daily or weekly diary so that all of us knew just exactly what the other was doing and what was needed. This has quite simply transformed my life! I now have a Mind Map on our fridge door and can visually see what the week ahead holds. It goes up at the weekend and we all do it together and add to it as the week progresses. I don't think my life has ever run so efficiently.'*

What my friend has demonstrated is that a Mind Map is a wonderful way to note down, in an attractive and organized way, everything you have to do. You can either have one overall Mind Map of the week ahead (with main branches for each day of the week, as my friend's Mind Map overleaf has) or a series of mini-Mind Maps that cover the areas of your future activities. These Mind Maps will give you a good degree of control over your future, and will help you plan far more easily and effectively.

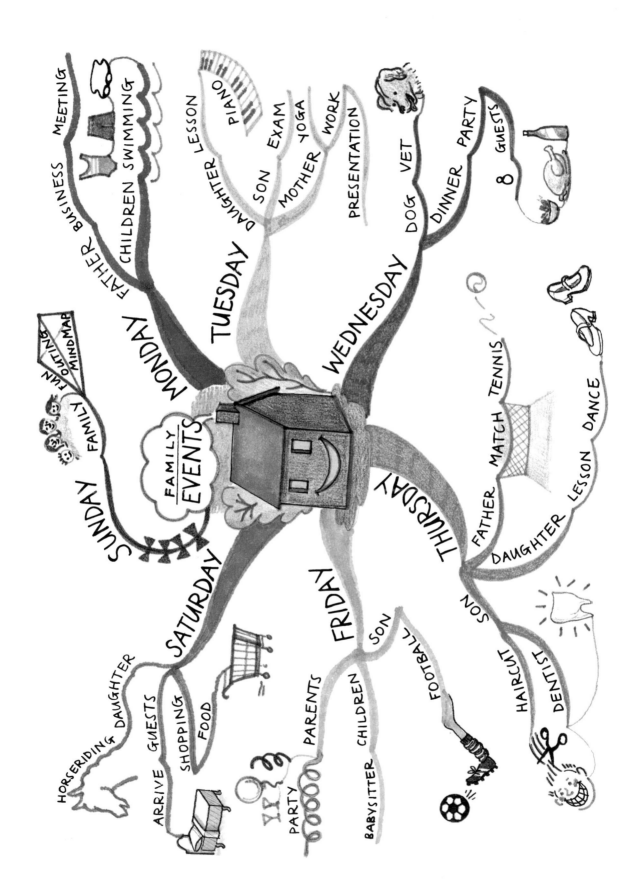

# PLANNING A BUDGET

Financial self-management is one area of life that gives many people a headache. Often people get into trouble because they are reluctant to look at their financial facts. They assume that things will take care of themselves, but live in constant fear of bills, credit-card statements, and those unexpected expenses that can strike out of the blue. It doesn't matter if you are comfortably off either – even people earning large salaries can invite disaster through inadequate financial planning.

The art of budgeting should be an essential part of your life. Budgeting is actually quite simple, once you get the hang of organizing yourself and your finances systematically. The trick is to make sure you know roughly when you will receive any money coming to you (your wages or salary, interest from savings accounts, state tax credits, pensions, maintenance, any dividends from shares you may have, etc.), and when you have to pay your regular bills.

A Mind Map will help you keep track of your regular expenses. Branch headings you could use for your Mind Map might include housing costs (rent, council tax, mortgage, etc.), insurance (car, health, contents), travel (season tickets, petrol), utilities (gas, water, electric), food, entertainment, and hobbies. You can add sub-branches detailing when each bill is due.

In this way you will easily be able to see how much and when you might have any surplus income over your expenditure, which you can save towards a holiday or your retirement.

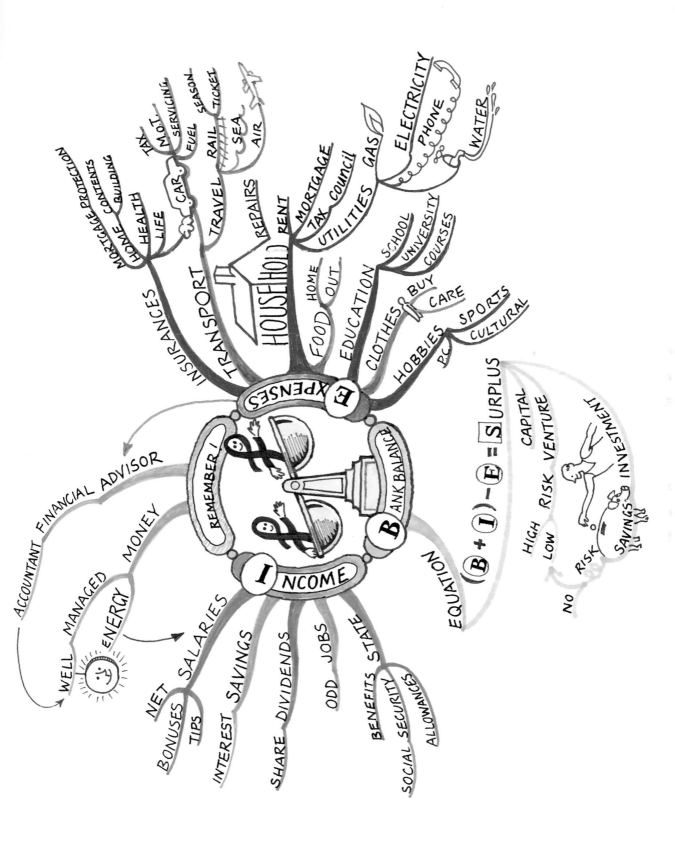

# CREATIVE PROBLEM SOLVING

Problems often have a habit of tying your mind up in knots! Every time you think about it, new bits of the problem appear, or solutions you've already thought of suddenly seem less than ideal, upon reflection.

If you're wrestling with such an intractable conundrum, a Mind Map can help light your way through the darkness.

From a central image representing the problem, radiate out branches defining exactly what is causing the problem to be such a headache, any possible solutions, where you might find help and/or professional advice, what the ideal solution would be from your point of view, and any circumstances that are restricting your options – money, time, other people, and so on.

All this will help clarify the problem and your possible solutions, and should allow you to make associations and linkages between different parts of the problem. You may find that one particular solution becomes associated with several different aspects of the problem – obviously this would need further exploration.

Often the simple act of writing a problem down will help get it into perspective. With Mind Maps, because they mimic the brain's own way of thinking round problems, you start with a huge advantage.

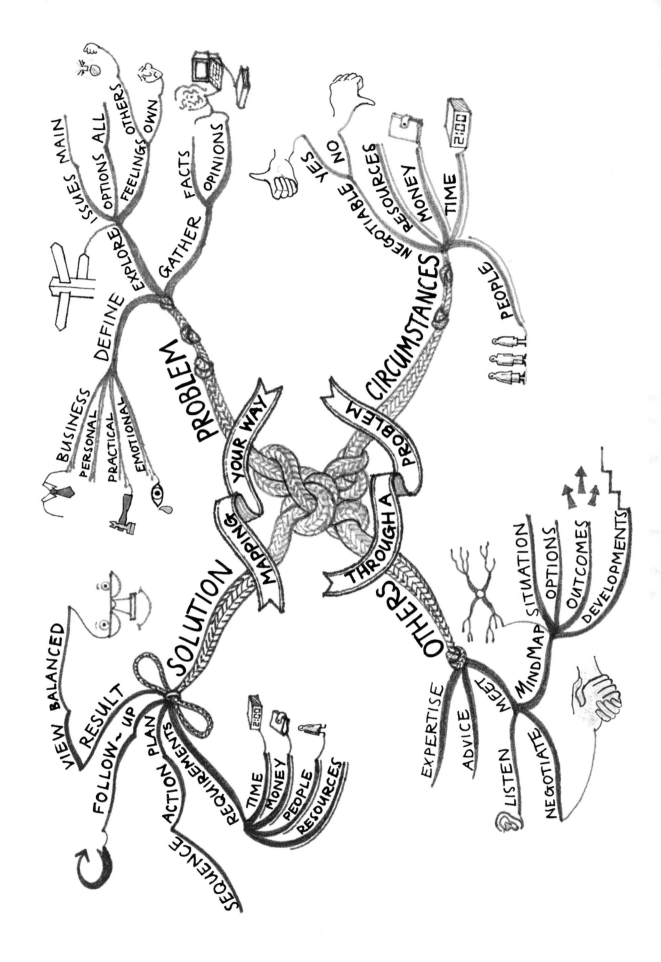

MAPPING YOUR WAY THROUGH A PROBLEM

PROBLEM
- DEFINE
  - BUSINESS
  - PERSONAL
  - PRACTICAL
  - EMOTIONAL
- EXPLORE
  - ISSUES MAIN
  - OPTIONS ALL
  - FEELINGS
    - OTHERS
    - OWN
- GATHER
  - FACTS
  - OPINIONS

CIRCUMSTANCES
- NEGOTIABLE
  - YES
  - ON
- RESOURCES
  - MONEY
  - TIME
- PEOPLE

SOLUTION
- VIEW BALANCED
- FOLLOW-UP
- RESULT
- ACTION PLAN
  - SEQUENCE
  - REQUIREMENTS
    - TIME
    - MONEY
    - PEOPLE
    - RESOURCES

OTHERS
- EXPERTISE
- ADVICE
- MEET
  - LISTEN
  - NEGOTIATE
- MINDMAP
  - SITUATION
  - OPTIONS
  - OUTCOMES
  - DEVELOPMENTS

# LIFE VISION AND PURPOSE

At some point in everyone's life events occur that prompt people to reassess their life vision: the birth of a child or grandchild, a serious illness, or (less dramatically) a career change or significant birthday. Such moments are often times of reflection and new resolution.

Take a little time now to sit down and think about your life vision.

What is important to you? Who is important to you? What are the values that you live by? What would you like to change in your life? What improvements would you like to make to your health/diet/outlook/education/social life?

Note your answers down on a Mind Map, and then think about how you can go about making those changes you want to make – going back to college, starting a fitness regime, eating more healthily, socializing more, keeping up with old friends more regularly.

Note the benefits a renewed life vision will bring you, such as more confidence, a better sense of where you're going, more energy, and greater happiness.

Pin up your completed Mind Map somewhere where you'll see it often, such as above your desk, or on your kitchen door.

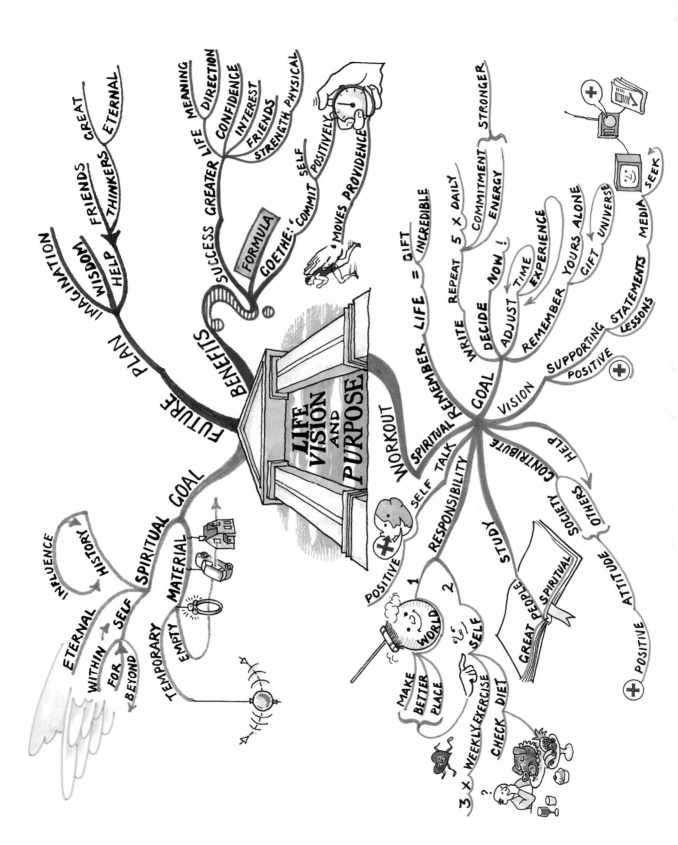

# CREATING YOUR IDEAL FUTURE

You have now become aware of the extraordinary power of Mind Maps. One other major use for them is to help you to take control of your future.

You will probably already be aware of the fact that 'you tend to get what you think you will get'. A Mind Map, as the most sophisticated thinking tool in the world, can help you think very well about what you want. Such a Mind Map will therefore significantly increase the probability that you will get it!

Your next and exciting task is, therefore, to let your imagination run riot! Imagine that you have limitless time, resources and energy, and that you can do anything that you wish, for all eternity. Again, using a large sheet of blank paper, and having a compact image in the centre that pictures, for you, the essence of your Ideal Future, develop a Mind Map (or ten!) on all those things you would like to accomplish if there were no limits placed upon your imagination.

This Ideal Future Mind Map should include all those things you have dreamed, at any stage in your life, of doing. Some of the most common dreams include travel, learning new languages, learning to play a musical instrument, drawing and painting, writing, learning new dances, exploring new subjects, and taking up new mental and physical sports and activities. (One useful way to prepare your brain to do this Mind Map is to do a quick speed Mind Map on everything you do not want in your ideal future.)

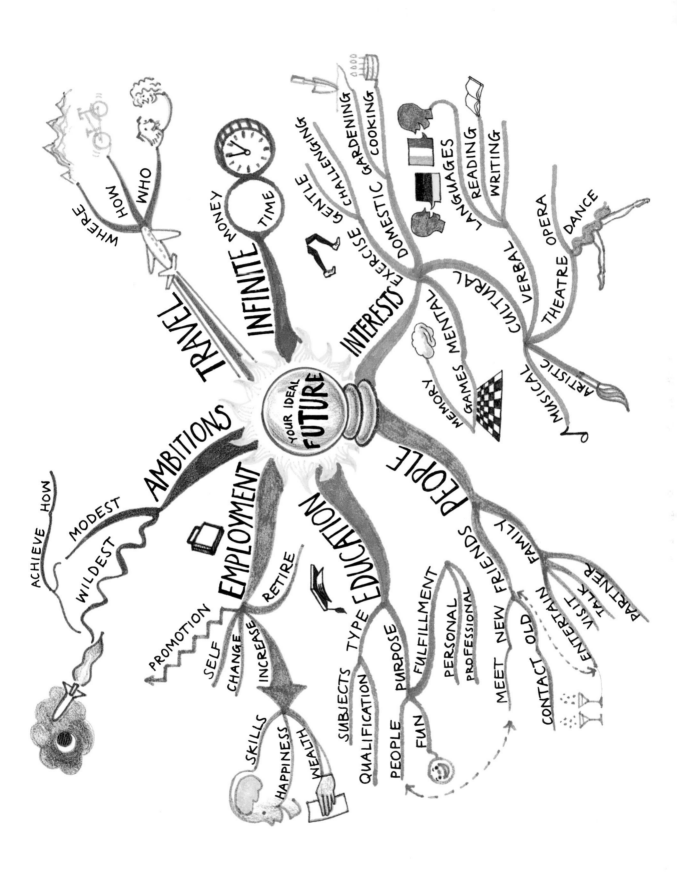

Suggested topics for your main branches include: Skills; Education; Friends; Family; Job; Hobbies; and Goals. Mind Map the rest of your life exactly as you would design it if a genie from a magic lamp had said to you that, if you Mind Mapped perfectly and extensively your ideal future, that genie would grant you every single wish!

When you are doing this Mind Map, make sure that you totally let your mind go, and Mind Map out everything you would truly like to do if you had that infinite time and money.

Include in this Mind Map as much colour and as many images as you can in order to stimulate your creative thinking.

One other useful mini-Mind Map you can create while Mind Mapping your Ideal Future is an ideal day in your future. Using a clock as your central image, Mind Map all the major elements of that perfect day. After you have completed that Mind Map, make that perfect day every day of your real life.

When you have completed your Ideal Future Mind Map, use it as a stimulus and guide to add quality and hope to the real future that you are going to both live and create. Decide that you'll make as much of it as possible come true. Many people who have already tried this Mind Map have found it to be extraordinarily successful in transforming their lives and making them more happy and successful. Within a few years (or less!) of creating their Mind Maps, they have found that as much as 80 percent of their dreams have come true!

# Afterword

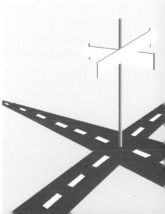

You are now in possession of *the* thinking tool which can transform the way you think for ever.

When you use Mind Maps on a daily basis, you will find that your life becomes more productive, fulfilled, and successful on every level:

→ You can achieve what you want to achieve.

→ You can become an ideas person.

→ You can become more efficient and more productive.

→ You can make your dreams a reality.

Like a road map, Mind Maps will help you get from where you are now to where you want to be.

As we have seen throughout this book, Mind Maps are so effective because they work *with* your brain and its natural ways of functioning: they are a physical realization of the incredible networking and explosive Mind Maps of thought in your head. In short, they work with the brain's all-important hunger for imagination and association. This is why Mind Mapping is a co-operative venture – and adventure – between what goes on in your head and what you put on paper.

As you now know, there are no limits to the number of thoughts, ideas, and connections that your brain can make, which means that there are no limits to the different ways you can use Mind Maps to help you.

I wish you every success and every enjoyment on your Mind Map journey with the universe of your brain.

# LEARNING AND THINKING FOR THE 21ST CENTURY

→ Make the Most of Your Mind

→ In-company Training

→ Licensing for Companies and Independent Trainers

→ 'Open' Business and Public Seminars

→ Educational Seminars

We are the **ONLY** organization that can license use of the Mind Maps and associated trademarks.

For full details of Buzan Learning Seminars and information on our range of BrainFriendly products, including:

→ Books

→ Software

→ Audio and video tapes

→ Support materials

**SEND FOR OUR BROCHURE**

**CONTACT US AT:**

Email: Buzan@BuzanCentres.com
Website: www.BuzanCentres.com

Or:

**Buzan Centres Ltd**
54 Parkstone Road
Poole, Dorset BH15 2PG
Telephone: +44 (0) 1202 674676
Fax: +44 (0) 1202 674776

**Buzan Centres Inc. (Americas)**
PO Box 4, Palm Beach
Florida
FL 33480, USA
Telephone (Free Toll in USA): +1 866 896 1024
Telephone: +1 734 207 5287

make the most of your mind today